THE FAITH FILES

Volume One:
The Gospels

John W. Stanko

purposequest
INK

The Faith Files–Volume One: The Gospels
by John W. Stanko
Copyright ©2008 John W. Stanko

Note: all bold text in Bible quotations are author's emphasis.

ISBN **978-1-63360-049-2**
For Worldwide Distribution
Printed in the U.S.A.

PurposeQuest Ink
P.O. Box 8882
Pittsburgh, PA 15221-0882
412.646.2780

Table of Contents

Other Evergreen Press books by John W. Stanko:

Life Is a Gold Mine: Can You Dig It?

I Wrote This Book on Purpose

A Daily Dose of Proverbs

So Many Leaders...So Little Leadership

Strictly Business

Unlocking the Power of Your Purpose

Beyond Purpose

INTRODUCTION

In 1995, I wrote my first book, *Life Is a Gold Mine: Can You Dig It?* In that book, I outlined and described what I consider the five "gold mine principles" of life, which are: purpose, goal-setting, time management, organization, and faith. I included faith because I felt it was the missing element in so many organizational and personal development seminars. After all, "without faith it is impossible to please him" (Hebrews 11:6).

At the end of the descriptions of principles in the book, I made some action-item recommendations for the reader. One of my recommendations after faith was to study every verse in the New Testament on faith, an ambitious task. When my publisher and I were preparing to revise and reprint *Gold Mine*, I read that recommendation, and it occurred to me that I was a hypocrite. I was asking others to do what I had never done—study everything the New Testament had to say about faith.

I thought studying New Testament faith would mostly involve looking at what Jesus and Paul said and wrote about faith. When I first did a search of every verse that included the words *faith, believe, believes, believed, believing, unbelieving, unbelief, doubt,* and *trust,* I was overwhelmed. I found that every New Testament author had something to say on the subject. Then I decided to jump in and study each passage to see what I could learn about faith. More importantly, I decided to see how I could *apply* what I had read and learned about faith.

In 2001, I began a weekly e-mail update called *The Monday Memo.* When I started my study of faith, I went to the *Monday Memo* readers (about 1,000 at the time) and asked if anyone wanted my notes on faith. To my surprise, people wrote to say they did. When I finished what came to be known as *The Faith*

Files, I continued my online studies and to date have completed a verse-by-verse devotional for eighteen books in the New Testament. It all began, however, with that recommendation to study faith that I finally decided to apply to my own life.

I'm not sure why I decided to call these *The Faith Files*; it seemed "cool," and I have never thought of any other name. These aren't files per se, but rather collections of faith stories and teaching passages with my thoughts on each. I have included questions that you can ask yourself that correspond to every passage and are designed to help you do what I did— apply the lesson(s) from that faith verse or story in your life right now. The questions are in bold so you can scan the pages and discover the questions with ease. Quality questions lead to a quality life, someone once said. If that's true, then I hope that these are quality faith questions that will lead to a quality personal faith for you and those you lead.

I decided to start with *The Faith Files* that look at what Jesus had to say about faith in the gospels. Jesus is the "author and finisher of our faith" (Hebrews 12:2). He is our ultimate faith focus, so He seemed like the logical starting point. I don't include many references to verses outside the gospels in this book because future editions will study faith in every other New Testament book and letter. I have tried to keep the focus on Jesus' words in this volume and will study the words of Paul, Peter, and John at a later date.

The format I use is simple and not meant to flow like most books. I include the passage in which each faith reference is used. Then I make a few points about what I saw or learned from that passage. While the passages are included in the order in which they appear, I want to avoid any concept that there is a system of faith in the gospels. Our great need isn't to *under-stand* faith; our need is to *apply* faith for daily living. Therefore, I want you to approach *The Faith Files* as an action devotional and not just a Bible study.

This book is an excellent tool for small group study as well as personal devotions. You don't have to follow the order of faith studies as I present them. Feel free to jump around from story to story or gospel to gospel.

Finally, I urge you to take notes in a journal as you respond to the questions I have included with each passage. Add your own insights to mine and keep expanding your understanding of faith, especially focusing on how to walk it out in your daily life. In fact, that is the byline for *The Faith Files: Increasing Your Faith for Daily Living.*

As you read, study, and grow in faith, I hope these exercises will do for you what they did for me. I started out with a simple study, and it led to so much more. Today 6,000 people all over the world receive my weekly Bible studies, and many use them to teach others. My study of faith led to a project much bigger than I first imagined. In other words, my faith led to action, which is the recurring theme throughout *The Faith Files.*

I invite you to join and read my ongoing weekly studies at www.stankobiblestudy.com. You can subscribe at that address to receive them directly, or you can stop by and visit when you have the time. I pray that you will enjoy *The Faith Files* and develop a hunger to find anything else that will help build your faith and equip you for action. If I can be of any further assistance, please don't hesitate to write me at johnstanko@att.net.

And now, let's begin by saying the simple invocation recited in many churches: "May the Lord bless the reading and study of His Word."

Dr. John W. Stanko
Pittsburgh, PA, USA
July 2008

Chapter One

The Gospel of Matthew

At one point in our marriage, my wife and I needed a new home. We thought the obstacle in our way was the home we had that we first needed to sell. Faith requires action, so we asked ourselves, "What can we *do* that would take us a step closer to our new home?" The answer was easy: put our house on the market to sell. And so we did.

After several months, nothing happened. So we asked ourselves the same question: "What can we *do*?" We decided the next step was to go out and look for a new house. After all, we reasoned, just looking didn't cost us anything.

To our surprise, we fell in love with the first house we saw. I can still remember our seven-year-old son running through the house saying, "Bless the Lord, oh my soul!" We went home confident that we had found our future home but unable to do anything until we sold our old one.

Another few weeks went by, and we asked ourselves that same question as to what we could *do*. We weren't experienced home buyers, but we decided to make an offer on the new house contingent upon selling the old one. The sellers accepted our bid, and we then had a deadline to sell the current home or the deal for the new house was off.

Over the next six weeks, we had only one East Indian family look at our house. They gave us a bid that was so low we didn't even counter offer. We thought they weren't serious. When we came to within a week of our deadline, we prayed as a family at the dinner table, "Lord, show us what we're not seeing here." Our four-year-old left the table and shortly came running back in to announce, "Daddy, the Indian family just drove by."

That was when I saw what we had not seen: we *had* sold our house, just not for the price we expected. I contacted our realtor and instructed her to make the best deal she could with the Indian family. She did and we sold our house just thirty-six hours before our deadline. There was only one remaining problem. We did not have the $10,000 down payment we needed to acquire the new home, since we had sold our house for much less than we had anticipated.

You may suspect what happened next. Someone gave us the money, and we closed on our new house that faith had made possible. I have come to realize that faith isn't so much an *event* as a *lifestyle*. We must learn to trust God for every situation and have faith that He will supply all of our needs. I have drawn lessons from that story for many years, and I thought I would tell it to you as we begin our study of faith in the gospels.

And now let's begin our study.

———————

Matthew wrote his gospel as a Jew to Jews to prove that Jesus, also a Jew, was the Messiah and Anointed One. Being the first gospel, Matthew gives us our first look at Jesus and His public ministry. **Faith** was one of the dominant themes in Jesus' public ministry. **Faith** is still a dominant theme for modern disciples. That is why we are studying faith and compiling *The Faith Files*.

Searching the NIV version of the Bible, I found that Matthew used the word *faith* fourteen times; *believe, believed,* and *believing* ten times; *unbelieving* once; and *doubt* twice, for a total of twenty-seven references to faith in his gospel.

Let's take a look at those references in context to see what we can learn about faith and how to apply it to our everyday lives.

1. **Matthew 6:30-34**—If that is how God clothes the grass of the field, which is here today and tomorrow is thrown into the fire, will he not much more clothe you, O you of little **faith**? So do not worry, saying, "What shall we eat?" or "What shall we drink?" or "What shall we wear?" For the pagans run after all these things, and your heavenly Father knows that you need them. But seek first his kingdom and his righteousness, and all these things will be given to you as well. Therefore do not worry about tomorrow, for tomorrow will worry about itself. Each day has enough trouble of its own.

• Jesus literally called the people "little faiths." He exhorted them not to worry about food, clothing, shelter, or the needs of tomorrow. (If Jesus were addressing people today, He would probably include transportation as well.) **Do you worry about your daily provision?** If so, you can stop. God promises to take care of you because He knows what you need.

• Worry is an indication of little faith. **Are you worrying at this time in your life? What about? How can you increase your faith for that particular problem?**

• The disciples were (and are) to seek first His kingdom. It is an evidence of faith that you have stopped seeking after your needs and are instead trusting God for them, seeking His will for your life first and foremost. To seek God's will implies that you *search* for it and then *do* it. **What is God's will and purpose for your life? Are you doing it? How can you do it more effectively?**

• Note that Jesus often asked people questions when He talked about faith. See Matthew 8:26, 9:28, 14:31, 16:8, and 21:25. **What is Jesus asking you about your faith?**

• This passage reports no miracles; it just records a basic teaching about faith. This is where faith begins in the gospels. **Can you get beyond your concern for and preoccupation with your own needs to do God's will?**

───·●·───

2. **Matthew 8:10, 13**—When Jesus heard this, he was astonished and said to those following him, "I tell you the truth, I have not found anyone in Israel with such great **faith**." Then Jesus said to the centurion, "Go! It will be done just as you **believed** it would." And his servant was healed at that very hour.

• The centurion came to the conclusion that Jesus could heal his servant. Perhaps you think that faith is something that you always feel. It is not. It is a gift from God that enables you to consider your need, as great as it may be, and then choose *not* to focus on the need but on God's ability to meet that need. While it is a gift, you must decide to receive it. When Jesus saw the centurion's decision to have faith, He was astonished. **When is the last time you astonished Jesus with your faith?**

• Jesus was not even present when the centurion's servant was healed. There is no human condition, need, sickness, or dilemma that is beyond the scope or touch of God's power. Don't limit what God can do by a preconceived notion of how He will do it. Just trust Him!

• Notice that faith brought diverse people to Jesus. Faith was not exclusively Jewish. As we see in Hebrews 11:6, faith is the *only* means by which anyone can come to God and consequently please Him. **Do you have God-pleasing faith? What is the evidence of such faith?**

3. **Matthew 8:24-26**—Without warning, a furious storm came up on the lake, so that the waves swept over the boat. But Jesus was sleeping. The disciples went and woke him, saying, "Lord, save us! We're going to drown!" He replied, "You of little **faith**, why are you so afraid?" Then he got up and rebuked the winds and the waves, and it was completely calm.

• Notice that storms arose when the disciples were with Jesus. **Do you notice this tendency in your life? How do you react to them? With fear or faith?**

• We see here that Jesus had faith. He doesn't ask you to do anything He hasn't already done. He was so calm that He went to sleep. Because Jesus had faith, He knows how to help you in your faith challenges.

• John Wesley, the founder of Methodism, was impacted by the Moravian believers on board his ship during a storm. **What impacted him?** He was impacted by their calm trust in the midst of bad weather. Your faith needs to become part of day-today life as you face storms. **What storms are you facing? Are you sleeping well in the midst of them?**

• This story clearly shows that God controls nature and natural causes. He is Lord over His creation; He speaks and it must obey. **Do you trust in God completely, no matter what you are facing? Do you know that you are just a word from God away from a solution to your problem?** Trust Him!

———————

4. **Matthew 9:1-2**—Jesus stepped into a boat, crossed over and came to his own town. Some men brought to him a paralytic, lying on a mat. When Jesus saw their **faith**, he said to the paralytic, "Take heart, son; your sins are forgiven."

• Jesus *saw* their faith, and He wants to see yours as well. James wrote, "Faith by itself, if it is not accompanied by action, is dead" (James 2:17). Faith is not evidenced by adhering to correct doctrine but rather acting in accordance with what you believe. **If you believe God is powerful, is that faith present in your everyday living? What faith steps are you taking to show that your faith is real?**

• They carried their friend to Jesus in faith. These men made a hole in a roof to get their friend or family member close to Jesus. It was their faith that healed him. He was not capable of saving or healing himself. **Is there anyone you need to carry to Jesus in faith? How can you do this?** Prayer is one answer that comes to mind. **Can you think of any other ways?**

• Notice their faith allowed the man's sins to be forgiven! There is no sin beyond God's forgiveness. **If God has forgiven**

you, have you forgiven yourself and others? Is there anyone that you have judged as too sinful to bring to God?

---

5. **Matthew 9:20-22**—Just then a woman who had been subject to bleeding for twelve years came up behind him and touched the edge of his cloak. She said to herself, "If I only touch his cloak, I will be healed." Jesus turned and saw her. "Take heart, daughter," he said, "your **faith** has healed you." And the woman was healed from that moment.

• The woman was afraid to touch Jesus. Operating in faith doesn't mean an absence of all doubt or fear. She didn't want to make Jesus unclean, which a woman with an issue of blood would do if she touched a man, according to the Law.

• Jesus felt something go out of Him, even though the crowd was pressing Him on every side. God knows you and what you need. He is not too busy to respond to you when you act in faith. He responds to *everyone* and *anyone* who touches Him in faith; He is never overwhelmed.

• Once again, we see that the woman did something—she took some action because of her faith. **What faith steps can you take today? Can you write a letter, make a phone call, write out a plan, or contact someone who can help you with your faith dream or faith need?**

• Notice also that Jesus said *He* had not healed her, but rather her *faith* had healed her. Her faith was what caused her to press through the crowd to touch Him. Therefore, it was her faith that was the ultimate means to her healing. Faith is the currency with which we make transactions with God. Your pockets are full of faith; make sure you spend it. When you spend it, however, you never lack, for your pockets are immediately refilled with even more than you previously had.

• The most difficult time to exercise faith is right after you've applied faith and seen God respond. Afterwards you can get cautious and not want to ask the Lord for too much. That is why I say it is the toughest time. **Are you in a cautious mode where your faith is concerned? What can you do to break out of it?**

———————

6. **Matthew 9:27-29**—As Jesus went on from there, two blind men followed him, calling out, "Have mercy on us, Son of David!" When he had gone indoors, the blind men came to him, and he asked them, "Do you **believe** that I am able to do this?" "Yes, Lord," they replied. Then he touched their eyes and said, "According to your **faith** will it be done to you."

• It seems that the burden of faith proof was on the two men. Jesus did not have to prove that He had the power to heal; they had to prove that they had the faith to be healed. Jesus determined that whatever they had faith to be done would be done. **If nothing is happening in your life, is it God's responsibility or a reflection of your faith level?**

• God is able to do what He said He will do. **Do you believe that? What are doing about what you believe?** These blind men *followed* Jesus and *cried out* to Him. They *answered* His questions. **What can you do to prove that you have faith? Do you see that this is the recurrent theme in faith encounters with Jesus?**

7. Matthew 13:53-58—When Jesus had finished these parables, he moved on from there. Coming to his hometown, he began teaching the people in their synagogue, and they were amazed. "Where did this man get this wisdom and these miraculous powers?" they asked. "Isn't this the carpenter's son? Isn't his mother's name Mary, and aren't his brothers James, Joseph, Simon and Judas? Aren't all his sisters with us? Where then did this man get all these things?" And they took offense at him. But Jesus said to them, "Only in his hometown and in his own house is a prophet without honor." And he did not do many miracles there because of their lack of **faith**.

• It is hard to believe that Jesus' ministry could be restricted in any way, but it was in Nazareth. **What restricted Him?** It was the people's lack of faith! **Where is your lack of faith limiting what God could do for you and others?**

• The people were both amazed and offended. They saw what He did, but they knew Him and His family so well that they could not make the connection.

• There may be some who are simply too familiar with you to receive who you are in Christ and what you can do. If that's the case, don't fret or waste any time trying to convince them. Let God lead you to those who can accept and receive. The apostle Paul encountered the same dynamic. His own people could not accept who he was in Christ and could only relate to him as they had in the past. **So what did God do?** The Lord took Paul to a people who did not know him in the past and could receive from him in the present.

8. Matthew 14:25-31—During the fourth watch of the night Jesus went out to them, walking on the lake. When the disciples saw him walking on the lake, they were terrified. "It's a ghost," they said, and cried out in fear. But Jesus immediately said to them: "Take courage! It is I. Don't be afraid." "Lord, if it's you," Peter replied, "tell me to come to you on the water." "Come," he said. Then Peter got down out of the boat, walked on the water and came toward Jesus. But when he saw the wind, he was afraid and, beginning to sink, cried out, "Lord, save me!" Immediately Jesus reached out his hand and caught him. "You of little **faith**," he said, "why did you **doubt**?"

• Peter acted boldly and courageously. He asked Jesus to prove that it was truly Him walking on the water. It's all right to ask God to prove Himself every now and then, especially if He is stretching your faith. We need to be careful, however, not to make it a habit.

• Jesus said to come, and Peter went. You have to give Peter credit for acting on his faith, even if it meant doing something that no one had seen anyone do until a minute earlier when Jesus approached. Faith takes you from the realm of the possible to the seemingly impossible. It takes you from the realm of the seen to the realm of the unseen and immaterial.

• It seems that Peter's fear caused him to doubt, and that led to him sinking. **Is it fair to say, then, that fear is the opposite of faith?** Someone once said that fear is the acronym for False Evidence Appearing Real. The false evidence here was that the wind was too much for Peter, and he would drown.

• Jesus asked Peter a question as to why he had little faith and doubted. Wow! Peter was walking on the water for a time but then began to sink. We can all identify with Peter, but Jesus seemed to rebuke him for his lack of faith.

• As I write, I am signing a contract to do 13 weeks of Internet radio for $6,700. I am excited, but I don't have the money, so I am also afraid. **What could you and I do if we weren't afraid?** I am determined to proceed and not fear, **but what if I fail? What if I don't have the money? What are you afraid of? What water could you walk on if it wasn't for your fear?**

———

9. **Matthew 15:22-28**—A Canaanite woman from that vicinity came to him, crying out, "Lord, Son of David, have mercy on me! My daughter is suffering terribly from demon-possession." Jesus did not answer a word. So his disciples came to him and urged him, "Send her away, for she keeps crying out after us." He answered, "I was sent only to the lost sheep of Israel." The woman came and knelt before him. "Lord, help me!" she said. He replied, "It is not right to take the children's bread and toss it to their dogs." "Yes, Lord," she said, "but even the dogs eat the crumbs that fall from their masters' table." Then Jesus answered, "Woman, you have great **faith**! Your request is granted." And her daughter was healed from that very hour.

• **Why did Jesus give this woman a difficult time**? Perhaps He was reflecting (but not sharing) the Jews' dislike for Gentiles, modeling how hard and cruel their attitude had made them. Certainly, the Jews did not believe that God wanted anything to do with a Gentile, unless they first became a Jew. They also felt the same about women, even if the women were Jewish!

• Maybe Jesus was testing this woman to see if she would persevere in her faith. This woman was desperate but had great faith in God. She did not take offense at the seeming harshness of the response to her initial request.

• Her daughter was healed without Jesus being present for her healing, just like the centurion's servant. Don't limit God and how He can act in response to your faith. Your faith can touch someone who happens to be far away from you physically because God can be where you can't.

• We see several instances when Jesus performed a miracle for Gentiles as an indication that the gospel would be available to *all* men and women. The disciples, however, missed the message and stayed in their Jewish culture and belief that faith in God was a Jewish commodity and privilege. **Is there any group that you think is beyond God's touch or help?** If there is, then you need to change your thinking!

10. **Matthew 16:6-8**—"Be careful," Jesus said to them. "Be on your guard against the yeast of the Pharisees and Sadducees." They discussed this among themselves and said, "It is because we didn't bring any bread." Aware of their discussion, Jesus asked, "You of little **faith**, why are you talking among yourselves about having no bread?"

• Their lack of faith caused the disciples to miss the lesson that Jesus was trying to teach them.

• **Is your lack of faith doing the same thing?**
• **Has Jesus proven His ability to provide for you? When? How?**
• **Why are you still worried?**
• **Why do you stop short of doing God's will? Is it because you don't believe He can meet your daily needs?**

• Remembering the past is one way to strengthen your faith today. God has never failed you, although He has seldom done things the way that you expected or according to your schedule. The disciples had just come from the meeting where Jesus had multiplied the loaves and fishes, yet they were fretting over not having brought any bread with them. **Have you done the same thing by fretting when God has just provided miraculously for you?**

———————

11. **Matthew 17:14-20**—When they came to the crowd, a man approached Jesus and knelt before him. "Lord, have mercy on my son," he said. "He has seizures and is suffering greatly. He often falls into the fire or into the water. I brought him to your disciples, but they could not heal him." "O **unbelieving** and perverse generation," Jesus replied, "how long shall I stay with you? How long shall I put up with you? Bring the boy here to me." Jesus rebuked the demon, and it came out of the boy, and he was healed from that moment. Then the disciples came to Jesus in private and asked, "Why couldn't we drive it out?" He replied, "Because you have so little **faith**. I tell you the truth, if you have **faith** as small as a mustard seed, you can say to this mountain, 'Move from here to there' and it will move. Nothing will be impossible for you."

• Notice that this father, along with the Canaanite woman in number nine above, came to Jesus and bowed down. Worship and belief, humility and faith, go hand in hand. **Do you see how helpless you are to help yourself? Then why worry over what you don't have the power to change?**

• **When nothing is happening, is it because God isn't doing anything, or is it because I don't have faith?** It seems that the impetus to cause something to happen is my faith, not God's willingness. God has shown He is willing.

• The disciples obviously didn't have faith the size of a small mustard seed, for the boy was not delivered until Jesus arrived. A mustard seed is small, so it doesn't take much faith to make a difference. So if I am not making a difference, that could mean I have *no* faith. Ouch!

• "Nothing will be impossible for you." That is not a source of pride or power but of humility. Faith is not a magic power but a means to connect us to God and His will. Your faith becomes the means by which you become God's power agent for change in this world. People should be glad when you show up with your faith. **Are they?**

• I have been speaking to my "mountains"—those insurmountable objects that seem to be blocking my view or path. I have *chosen* to believe that God can move them, using anyone as a means to do it. **What are you doing with the mountains in your life? Climbing them? Admiring them? Complaining about them? Or casting them into the sea, in a manner of speaking?**

12. **Matthew 18:6**—But if anyone causes one of these little ones who **believe** in me to sin, it would be better for him to have a large millstone hung around his neck and to be drowned in the depths of the sea.

• Believing in Jesus is not mere mental assent but putting complete trust, confidence, and reliance in Him. Too often, I hear people say, "I believe in God." I want to respond, "So what? What difference has it made in your life?" **If you believe in God, shouldn't it impact your giving, relationships, and attitudes?**

• **What about you? Do you believe in Jesus? If so, how would someone know that if he or she was examining your life? Do you rely upon Him for what you need, what you do, and who you are?**

• I don't want to put any obstacle in the path of anyone I meet who believes (trusts, has confidence in, relies on—whatever word you use) God. I want to be careful not to complicate or damage someone else's simple faith in God.

13. **Matthew 21:18-22**—Early in the morning, as he was on his way back to the city, he was hungry. Seeing a fig tree by the road, he went up to it but found nothing on it except leaves. Then he said to it, "May you never bear fruit again!" Immediately the tree withered. When the disciples saw this, they were amazed. "How did the fig tree wither so quickly?" they asked. Jesus replied, "I tell you the truth, if you have **faith** and do not **doubt,** not only can you do what was done to the fig tree, but also you can say to this mountain, 'Go, throw yourself into

the sea,' and it will be done. If you **believe**, you will receive whatever you ask for in prayer."

• I don't fully understand this. I receive whatever I ask in prayer *if* I believe. This promise has a condition: I must have faith to get from God what I am asking. Jesus seems to have emphasized our personal responsibility in the faith process.

• **Can't this be abused? What does it mean when I don't receive my requests? Should I keep praying? Does it represent lack of faith? Does the existence of any doubt nullify my faith? Is this faith a gift from God or a decision of my will?**

• I know that this story must be considered in the context of what happened next: Jesus cursed the Jewish "fig tree" that looked good and religious but was not bearing any fruit acceptable to God. **Who would have thought that God would bring down the whole Jewish system of worship and life forty years later by destroying the temple and Jerusalem?** He did indeed figuratively curse their fig tree. God speaks and things happen!

• When I speak, things should happen too! My words are a reflection of my faith.

• This verse must be studied *along with* all other verses on faith. It is not the only statement that Jesus made about the subject. Be careful not to build a doctrinal case or practice based on only one verse or passage.

• My lack of faith is a root cause of my lack of prayer and, consequently, my lack of *answers* to prayer. The problem is not God's; it's mine!

• I don't declare the miracles that God can do as often as I should. I'm also not praying prayers that are big enough. Furthermore, I'm not asking God to do all that He can do. I'm focusing on unimportant, small things when God wants me to focus on major things. **Do you have that same tendency? If so, what are you prepared to do about it?**

———————

14. **Matthew 21:23-27**—Jesus entered the temple courts, and, while he was teaching, the chief priests and the elders of the people came to him. "By what authority are you doing these things?" they asked. "And who gave you this authority?" Jesus replied, "I will also ask you one question. If you answer me, I will tell you by what authority I am doing these things. John's baptism— where did it come from? Was it from heaven, or from men?" They discussed it among themselves and said, "If we say, 'From heaven,' he will ask, 'Then why didn't you **believe** him?' But if we say, 'From men'—we are afraid of the people, for they all hold that John was a prophet." So they answered Jesus, "We don't know." Then he said, "Neither will I tell you by what authority I am doing these things."

• The leaders chose not to have faith. **Do you see the rationale in their deliberations?** This proves that faith is something that you think about, consider, and then do. It made sense to them not to believe in John's mission or ministry—they had too much to lose. So they refused to answer His question.

• You can make rational decisions based on faith. For instance, you can think, "God is able to provide for me. This person has a need, and I choose to give what I have right now." That is rational faith!

• You can hear the fear in the leaders' deliberations. They were afraid of both the people and losing their position. In some sense, they were afraid just like Peter was when he was walking on the water. Fear causes you to make bad faith decisions. **Are you making any bad faith decisions lately?** Then don't look for unfaith, look for fear in your life. **Is fear the opposite of faith?**

---

15. **Matthew 21:28-32**—"What do you think? There was a man who had two sons. He went to the first and said, 'Son, go and work today in the vineyard.' 'I will not,' he answered, but later he changed his mind and went. Then the father went to the other son and said the same thing. He answered, 'I will, sir,' but he did not go. Which of the two did what his father wanted?" "The first," they answered. Jesus said to them, "I tell you the truth, the tax collectors and the prostitutes are entering the kingdom of God ahead of you. For John came to you to show you the way of righteousness, and you did not **believe** him, but the tax collectors and the prostitutes did. And even after you saw this, you did not repent and **believe** him."

• Jesus rebuked the leaders for not believing, especially in light of what Jesus Himself had been doing. God had given them another chance to believe after they had rejected John. They were stubbornly clinging to their unbelief even when the unrighteous such as the prostitutes and tax gatherers in their midst had chosen to believe in Jesus.

• Sometimes to have faith today, you must repent for what you believed yesterday. There is nothing wrong with having misplaced your trust, but it is wrong to cling to it when God shows you something better. I expect to grow in faith and abandon things I once believed. For instance, I formerly believed that God would work predominantly in my life through a pastor or man of God. I have repented of that belief and now trust God to do what I thought could only happen through a human agency. **When is the last time you changed what you believed for the good? Do you think that is a healthy step to take?**

• The prostitutes and tax gatherers had faith, and God accepted them. Don't discount anyone because of their past once they start to exercise faith. God doesn't judge by externals but by the heart. God knows those who have faith and those who don't. Jesus could speak with confidence that those who appeared most likely to have faith (the leaders) did *not* have it. God knows those who have faith.

---

16. **Matthew 24:23-28**—"At that time if anyone says to you, 'Look, here is the Christ!' or, 'There he is!' do not **believe** it. For false Christs and false prophets will appear and perform great signs and miracles to deceive even the elect—if that were possible. See, I have told you ahead of time. So if anyone tells you, 'There he is, out in the desert,' do not go out; or, 'Here he is, in the inner rooms,' do not **believe** it. For as lightning that comes from the east is visible even in the west, so will be the coming of the Son of Man. Wherever there is a carcass, there the vultures will gather."

• **Why is there counterfeit faith in circulation?** There is counterfeit faith for the same reason there are counterfeit $20 bills in circulation—because there are real $20 bills! No one in his or her right mind would accept a $3 bill. The reason there are counterfeit messiahs in whom people place their faith is because there was and is a real Messiah—Jesus.

• False messiahs are simply proof that there is a real one. It is our job to spread the word that there is only one and urge people to attach their inevitable faith in the right Messiah. **Why do I say "inevitable faith"?** Faith is a fact of life. Everyone has faith and puts it somewhere or in something. It may be in capitalism, a motivational speaker, a life doctrine like communism, or in another person's abilities (or their own). Everyone exercises faith; the only faith that leads to eternal life, however, is in Jesus.

---

17. **Matthew 27:41-44**—In the same way the chief priests, the teachers of the law and the elders mocked him. "He saved others," they said, "but he can't save himself! He's the King of Israel! Let him come down now from the cross, and we will **believe** in him. He **trusts** in God. Let God rescue him now if he wants him, for he said, 'I am the Son of God.'" In the same way, the robbers who were crucified with him also heaped insults on him.

• The Jews wanted a sign that didn't come from a sincere search but from a mocking unbelief! They had seen Jesus accomplish so much, and now they wanted a show, not a confirmation for faith. If He had come down from the cross, they would have been as afraid as Peter was when he tried to walk on the water. God may honor a sincere request for a faith confirmation that will build trust, but He resisted then and resists now a divine show that would provide entertainment at best. **What**

sign are you waiting for before you will do something that God has laid on your heart to do?

• Be cautious when you ask for a sign to help your faith, remembering that Jesus was raised from the dead. It would be hard to provide a more significant sign than that. If you can believe that God raises the dead, you have all you need to have faith today. **What can you believe God for today based on the fact that He raises the dead?**

• Although they were mocking Jesus, notice the testimony that the Jews gave about Him. They indicated that Jesus had trust in the Father. Jesus isn't asking us to do anything He didn't do. He died on the cross in faith, entrusting Himself to the Father, knowing the Father would not abandon Him. Up to that point, He had lived a life of faith. **Are you prepared to do the same, just as Jesus did? Are you ready to ask Him for help to do so?**

CONCLUSION

Matthew had a lot to say about faith, don't you agree? **If you have chosen to follow the order of faith references, what stands out most from your study of Matthew?** Review your notes and be diligent to apply your action steps in the coming days and weeks. Don't be in a hurry to move on, but also don't delay in taking faith steps. I have found that most people know exactly what they must do, and they have been considering those actions for quite some time. **Is that true in your case?**

Don't hesitate to talk to someone you trust about what you are considering but be careful whom you choose. Make sure they will encourage and not discourage faith.

Chapter Two

The Gospel of Mark

A number of years ago, my wife went to the doctor for what we thought was a routine checkup. When she left the doctor's office, she called me right away to let me know that the doctor had found a mass in her abdomen the size of a grapefruit. He had no idea what it was, but he scheduled tests two weeks later. I thought it was strange that he wanted to wait that long for the tests, but I knew we could put the time to good use.

The first thing we did was eliminate caffeine and junk food from our diet. We also fasted for part of the two weeks. Every time I walked past my wife, I cursed that tumor in the name of Jesus. I talked to it as if it were a living person, told it that it was not welcome in the house or my wife's body, and told it that it had to go.

I had my wife sit in a chair, and I positioned a music player right next to her abdomen. We played worship music into her stomach, and I would say, "This is the music we like. If you want to stay, you will have to listen to this music."

When the time came for my wife's tests, I was so confident that God healed her that I didn't even go to the doctor's office with her. (I would not do that again today.) When she was done, she called to say that the doctor had no idea what had happened. He assumed he had made a mistake before, although he knew what he had felt. There was no mass in my wife's abdomen. She was healed.

Did we exhibit bizarre behavior? We did. Would I take the same steps today? I'm not sure. I am sure of one thing, however, and that is that Jesus healed and God heals. I preached a message from that experience entitled, "Just Because the Postman Rings Your Bell Doesn't Mean You Have to Sign for the Package." I felt that the doctor tried to give us a bad report, and we rejected the report, vigorously and with faith.

We will observe Jesus healing in Mark's gospel just as He did in Matthew's. I don't believe that God only healed 2,000 years ago. He still heals today. Remember, your goal as you read *The Faith Files* isn't simply to learn more *about faith*. Your goal is to learn *how to apply your faith* to everyday life situations and problems.

And now let's continue with our study of God's Word and what it has to say about faith in Mark's gospel.

———————

Many believe that Mark was Peter's assistant in ministry. This gospel, therefore, could be Peter's account of his life with Jesus, as Mark heard it reported on numerous occasions. It is the shortest gospel and moves quickly and with urgency through the various stories and teachings.

Using the NIV version as a reference, I found that Mark uses the word *faith* seven times; *believe, believes, and believing* 16 times; *unbelieving and unbelief* once each; and *doubt* once, for a total of twenty-six *faith* references in this gospel. Let's study those references now to add to what we learned in Matthew's gospel about faith and how to apply it to daily life.

1. **Mark 1:15**—"The time has come," he said. "The kingdom of God is near. Repent and **believe** the good news!"

• The Amplified Bible always translates faith with the words "trust in, rely on and adhere to." You may want to inject those words into some of these verses when you see the words *faith* or *believe*.

• The Kingdom is the government of God, which is God ruling through the faith of His people. **Is that a correct statement? Or does that make God's government too dependent on man's faith? After all, God rules whether I have faith or not. Or does He? Will God act apart from our faith?**

• **What is the connection between repentance, faith, and the gospel (good news)? Is our initial act of repentance that leads to salvation repentance for our lack of faith in God? Is that our sin condition that plagues all of mankind?**

———————

2. **Mark 2:1-12**—A few days later, when Jesus again entered Capernaum, the people heard that he had come home. So many gathered that there was no room left, not even outside the door, and he preached the word to them. Some men came, bringing to him a paralytic, carried by four of them. Since they could not get him to Jesus because of the crowd, they made an opening in the roof above Jesus and, after digging through it, lowered the mat the paralyzed man was lying on.

When Jesus saw their **faith**, he said to the paralytic, "Son, your sins are forgiven." Now some teachers of the law were sitting there, thinking to themselves, "Why does this fellow talk like that? He's blaspheming! Who can forgive sins but God alone?" Immediately Jesus knew in his spirit that this was what they were thinking in their hearts, and he said to them, "Why are you thinking these things? Which is easier: to say to the paralytic, 'Your sins are forgiven,' or to say, 'Get up, take your mat and walk'? But that you may know that the Son of Man has authority on earth to forgive sins...." He said to the paralytic, "I tell you, get up, take your mat and go home." He got up, took his mat and walked out in full view of them all. This amazed everyone and they praised God, saying, "We have never seen anything like this!"

• Jesus *saw* their faith when they carried their friend and dug through the roof. Faith, if not accompanied by action, is useless. **Does Jesus see your faith? If so, in what way or in what part of your life? Are you trusting God for something that, unless He comes through, will make you look like a fool?**

• People praised and worshiped God because they saw faith in action, both on the part of the four men who carried the paralytic and from Jesus. They saw a life radically changed through faith in the power of God (through the men), and they saw the power of God (through Jesus' actions). **Is your faith a source of worship for other people? Do people praise God due in part to your influence?**

• When faith is working, we will see wonders we have never seen before. When our faith works, we work, as we "carry" something or someone to God, dig a hole in the roof, teach people, dispute cynics, forgive sins, or carry pallets and go home. Notice that everyone was doing something in this passage! **What are you doing with or in faith?**

3. **Mark 4:35-41**—That day when evening came, he said to his disciples, "Let us go over to the other side." Leaving the crowd behind, they took him along, just as he was, in the boat. There were also other boats with him. A furious squall came up, and the waves broke over the boat, so that it was nearly swamped. Jesus was in the stern, sleeping on a cushion. The disciples woke him and said to him, "Teacher, don't you care if we drown?" He got up, rebuked the wind and said to the waves, "Quiet! Be still!" Then the wind died down and it was completely calm. He said to his disciples, "Why are you so afraid? Do you still have no **faith**?" They were terrified and asked each other, "Who is this? Even the wind and the waves obey him!"

• Going over to the other side of the lake was Jesus' idea. He started that faith journey, and He has started yours as well. (Remember, He is the author of our faith; see Hebrews 12:1). The trouble you may be encountering now isn't your doing; it is God's! Neither have you made a mistake, nor is God angry with you. He has put you into what is known as a test or trial.

• The disciples were afraid *during* the storm and they were terrified *after* the storm—first because of the fury of the wind, then because of the power of God. We seek God's presence, but it can be terrifying. **Are you really ready for God to do miraculous things with and through you?**

• All of creation obeys God's voice. After Jesus spoke, the winds and waves calmed down. It's almost as if this storm had a personality of its own. He spoke to it as one would speak to another person. **Could this have been a demonically-inspired storm? Is it Satan whom Jesus was addressing?** Regardless, this text is proof that Jesus was and is God. For us, weather is either delightful or terrifying. For Him, it was just another aspect of His creation that was under His control.

• Jesus asked, "Do you still have no faith?" God has given us evidence of His power and goodness to build our faith. We must remember what He has done as we face new storms and pressures. At some point, God expects us to have faith and face and overcome our fears. **Are you using yesterday's faith victories to face today's faith challenges?**

• Don't mistake God's inaction to mean that He doesn't care for you. He does.

———

4. **Mark 5:25-34**—And a woman was there who had been subject to bleeding for twelve years. She had suffered a great deal under the care of many doctors and had spent all she had, yet instead of getting better she grew worse. When she heard about Jesus, she came up behind him in the crowd and touched his cloak, because she thought, "If I just touch his clothes, I will be healed." Immediately her bleeding stopped and she felt in her body that she was freed from her suffering. At once Jesus realized that power had gone out from him. He turned around in the crowd and asked, "Who touched my clothes?" "You see the people crowding against you," his disciples answered, "and yet you can ask, 'Who touched me?'" But Jesus kept looking around to see who had done it. Then the woman, knowing what had happened to her, came and fell at his feet and, trembling with fear, told him the whole truth. He said to her, "Daughter, your **faith** has healed you. Go in peace and be freed from your suffering."

• Here was a secret act of faith (the woman approached Jesus anonymously) that was recognized and publicly rewarded.

• Notice the logic in the woman's approach. Starting in faith, she acted rationally—"If I can just touch Him, I will be healed." She decided to have faith and acted. **Where and how can you decide to have faith today and act on it?**

• This woman was healed not by Jesus saying anything, but by the essence of who He was. He did not lay hands on her; she just touched Him.

• Jesus did three things for her: 1) healed her or made her whole, 2) freed her from her suffering, and 3) sent her away in peace. God is able to do exceedingly abundantly beyond all we can ask or think! (see Ephesians 3:20 NKJV). She wanted to be healed, but Jesus made her whole and gave her peace as well.

• Jesus didn't know who touched Him, yet He knew someone did. **What did He feel? What flowed out of Him that He felt it go?** When Paul told us (see Philippians 2:6-11) that Jesus emptied Himself to become a servant, we know that Jesus was still fully God while fully man. God is never diminished in any way when He acts on behalf of His people. So don't act as if He is diminished by limiting your faith requests.

———

5. **Mark 5:21-24, 36-43**—When Jesus had again crossed over by boat to the other side of the lake, a large crowd gathered around him while he was by the lake. Then one of the synagogue rulers, named Jairus, came there. Seeing Jesus, he fell at his feet and pleased earnestly with him, "My little daughter is dying. Please come and

you're your hands on her so that she will be healed and live." So Jesus went with him. A large crowd followed and pressed around him.... Ignoring what they said, Jesus told the synagogue ruler, "Don't be afraid; just **believe**." He did not let anyone follow him except Peter, James and John the brother of James.

When they came to the home of the synagogue ruler, Jesus saw a commotion, with people crying and wailing loudly. He went in and said to them, "Why all this commotion and wailing? except Peter, Peter, James and John the brother of James. The child is not dead but asleep." But they laughed at him. After he put them all out, he took the child's father and mother and the disciples who were with him, and went in where the child was. He took her by the hand and said to her, "*Talitha koum!*" (which means, "Little girl, I say to you, get up!"). Immediately the girl stood up and walked around (she was twelve years old). At this they were completely astonished. He gave strict orders not to let anyone know about this, and told them to give her something to eat.

• Jesus urged the synagogue ruler to ignore what the people were saying and to ignore being ridiculed. Jesus made the statement that the girl was not dead, only asleep.

• Faith gave Jesus a different perspective that she was only asleep, not dead. **Does God want to change how you see some situation that is now in your life?** He can do that when you put your trust in God's faith perspective rather than in your own limited perspective. At times, faith does seem to be illogical, although walking and acting in faith is the epitome of logic.

• Faith does not seek to create a spectacle, but seeks to do good through the power of God. Jesus didn't show off what He had done. He didn't make the little girl fall down or use her to encourage others to have faith by having her jump up and down to prove that her healing was real. Jesus simply told them to give her something to eat and ordered them not to tell anyone. He didn't go back to the crowd and say, "See, I told you she was asleep." Jesus wasn't interested in His reputation or proving He was correct. He was sent to help people have faith and that is what He did!

---

6. **Mark 6:1-6**—Jesus left there and went to his hometown, accompanied by his disciples. When the Sabbath came, he began to teach in the synagogue, and many who heard him were amazed. "Where did this man get these things?" they asked. "What's this wisdom that has been given him, that he even does miracles! Isn't this the carpenter? Isn't this Mary's son and the brother of James, Joseph, Judas and Simon? Aren't his sisters here with us?" And they took offense at him. Jesus said to them, "Only in his hometown, among his relatives and in his own house is a prophet without honor." He could not do any miracles there, except lay his hands on a few sick people and heal them. And he was amazed at their lack of **faith**. Then Jesus went around teaching from village to village.

• The Lord was surprised by their lack of faith. I assume that He would still be amazed at the lack of faith among some of His followers. He is amazed that people would rather sit in unbelief than receive the blessings that God can bestow. Perhaps He is amazed because that idea is so illogical.

30

• Jesus could not do any miracles. It seems once again that our lack of faith limits what God can do. **Where is your lack of faith limiting what God can do in and for you?**

• Because the people knew Jesus, they took offense at Him. He came home and wanted to help those He knew best and had grown up with, but they could not overcome their bias. No wonder it was said in Israel that no good came out of Nazareth. They were not worthy of Jesus. **Is that why He moved to Capernaum?** *Oh Lord, don't move from me because I don't welcome You and what You can do in my life!*

• It can be hard to receive from someone you know well. Don't let familiarity prevent you from receiving what God has for you through someone close to you. Don't put your faith in the person or their limitations; put your faith in God!

———

7. **Mark 9:15-29**—As soon as all the people saw Jesus, they were overwhelmed with wonder and ran to greet him. "What are you arguing with them about?" he asked. A man in the crowd answered, "Teacher, I brought you my son, who is possessed by a spirit that has robbed him of speech. Whenever it seizes him, it throws him to the ground. He foams at the mouth, gnashes his teeth and becomes rigid. I asked your disciples to drive out the spirit, but they could not." "O **unbelieving** generation," Jesus replied, "how long shall I stay with you? How long shall I put up with you? Bring the boy to me." So they brought him. When the spirit saw Jesus, it immediately threw the boy into a convulsion. He fell to the ground and rolled around, foaming at the mouth. Jesus asked the boy's father,

"How long has he been like this?" "From childhood," he answered. "It has often thrown him into fire or water to kill him. But if you can do anything, take pity on us and help us." "'If you can'?" said Jesus. "Everything is possible for him who **believes**." Immediately the boy's father exclaimed, "I do **believe**; help me overcome my **unbelief**!"

When Jesus saw that a crowd was running to the scene, he rebuked the evil spirit. "You deaf and mute spirit," he said, "I command you, come out of him and never enter him again." The spirit shrieked, convulsed him violently and came out. The boy looked so much like a corpse that many said, "He's dead." But Jesus took him by the hand and lifted him to his feet, and he stood up. After Jesus had gone indoors, his disciples asked him privately, "Why couldn't we drive it out?" He replied, "This kind can come out only by prayer."

• This is one of my favorite faith accounts because the father was so transparent with Jesus, and Jesus was so accepting of where the father was. Jesus did not rebuke the father for his lack of faith; Jesus accepted him where he was and still did the deed the father asked Him to do. The father must have had faith at least the size of a mustard seed.

•Everything is possible for those who have faith. **Everything? Then why don't some things happen for which I think I have faith?**

•This father's honesty is refreshing. "I believe, help me where I don't believe." His confession that he had doubt didn't prevent Jesus from doing what the father had asked. Your doubts won't either, if you don't let them rule what you do. You don't have to deny your doubts to talk or come to God.

• While the boy is thrashing on the ground and foaming at the mouth, Jesus entered into a discussion with the boy's father. Jesus was so calm during situations that could easily unnerve you and me.

• Jesus told the disciples that this kind of demon only came out through prayer. **Why?** Because the symptoms—throwing him down or into a fire, foaming at the mouth—seemed to point to epilepsy. The boy, however, actually had a deaf and dumb spirit! Jesus was saying that spiritual insight was required to deliver the boy from the root cause and not just the apparent symptoms.

• Jesus commanded the spirit never to enter the boy again. That means that the spirit would have tried to come back had Jesus not forbidden it to do so.

---

8. **Mark 9:42-48**—"And if anyone causes one of these little ones who **believe** in me to sin, it would be better for him to be thrown into the sea with a large millstone tied around his neck. If your hand causes you to sin, cut it off. It is better for you to enter life maimed than with two hands to go into hell, where the fire never goes out. And if your foot causes you to sin, cut it off. It is better for you to enter life crippled than to have two feet and be thrown into hell. And if your eye causes you to sin, pluck it out. It is better for you to enter the kingdom of God with one eye than to have two eyes and be thrown into hell, where 'their worm does not die, and the fire is not quenched.'"

• Tampering or hindering someone's faith is a serious offense according to Jesus. It would be better to do yourself bodily harm than to weaken anyone's faith. Of course, Jesus is not advocating mutilation but rather communicating that building up another's faith is a high priority in God's eyes. Not building up faith, therefore, is hindering the work and will of God for someone else.

• **So the question is: How can I weaken another's faith?** I can think of a few ways: 1) pessimism; 2) judging or criticizing someone's actions; 3) not sharing a testimony that could encourage someone's faith; 4) not allowing someone to make faith mistakes, insisting instead on perfection. (Remember, even Peter sank when he tried to walk on the water, but he was the only one who at least tried.) **Can you think of any other ways to hinder someone else's faith?**

• Remember, hindering or weakening someone's faith is serious business, so try not to do it. If you do, try to correct your deed as quickly as possible.

———————

9. **Mark 10:46-52**—Then they came to Jericho. As Jesus and his disciples, together with a large crowd, were leaving the city, a blind man, Bartimaeus (that is, the Son of Timaeus), was sitting by the roadside begging. When he heard that it was Jesus of Nazareth, he began to shout, "Jesus, Son of David, have mercy on me!" Many rebuked him and told him to be quiet, but he shouted all the more, "Son of David, have mercy on me!" Jesus stopped and said, "Call him." So they called to the blind man, "Cheer up! On your feet! He's calling you." Throwing his cloak aside, he jumped to his feet

and came to Jesus. "What do you want me to do for you?" Jesus asked him. The blind man said, "Rabbi, I want to see." "Go," said Jesus, "your **faith** has healed you." Immediately he received his sight and followed Jesus along the road.

• Bartimaeus couldn't see, but he could hear! He used what he had to get hold of God. Don't be hindered by your limitations. Use what you have with where you are to seek the Lord. **Where you have you let your limitations become a focus that has hindered your faith?**

• The "ushers" told him to be quiet. I have often tried to protect God so he would not be bothered by pushy or needy people! What a silly man I am! We need those who will "usher" people into the presence of God, not out of it!

• This blind man ignored those who told him to be quiet. God used these people to help focus his faith; He wouldn't take no for an answer! We shouldn't either. **Where have you taken no for an answer? How can you renew your faith in that area?**

• This man was blind and a beggar, up to that point in his life only having faith that people would take pity on him and give him alms. Without faith, you and I are reduced to beggars as well! We are reduced to finding help that is really no help at all. God is the only source of true help for our spiritual and physical needs. **Is there any area in which you are a beggar and not a faith carrier?**

• It seems obvious what this man would have wanted Jesus to do, but Jesus still made him verbalize it. We must be specific and clear about what we want God to do.

• Bartimaeus was healed immediately, not gradually, and he followed Jesus without delay. He knew that he had found the source, and he wasn't going to let Jesus out of his sight!

• Jesus said that the blind man's faith healed him. We see once again that our faith plays a role in what we receive from God. **Where has your faith limited what God can do for you and yours?**

10. **Mark 11:20-25**—In the morning, as they went along, they saw the fig tree withered from the roots. Peter remembered and said to Jesus, "Rabbi, look! The fig tree you cursed has withered!" "Have **faith** in God," Jesus answered. "I tell you the truth, if anyone says to this mountain, 'Go, throw yourself into the sea,' and does not doubt in his heart but believes that what he says will happen, it will be done for him. Therefore I tell you, whatever you ask for in prayer, **believe** that you have received it, and it will be yours. And when you stand praying, if you hold anything against anyone, forgive him, so that your Father in heaven may forgive you your sins."

• I have found it helpful if I visualize the answer for which I am praying. It helps me focus my faith. I try to see it as already done and then imagine how I will feel when the answer comes.

• **What does this passage tell us about the relationship between faith and prayer? Faith and forgiveness? Prayer and forgiveness?**

• **Is it possible to have faith in faith? Faith in your ability**

to get God to act? Faith in prayer? Our faith must be in God and not any technique or discipline, no matter how spiritual the technique or formula seems to be!

• Notice that they stood when they prayed—face to face with God, in a position of readiness to carry out His will.

———

11. **Mark 15:32**—"Let this Christ, this King of Israel, come down now from the cross, that we may see and **believe**." Those crucified with him also heaped insults on him.

• Unbelief says, "Show me and I'll believe." Faith says, "I believe, show me."

• Jesus hung on the cross, having faith that His Father would raise Him from the dead.

• People insulted and mocked Jesus for His faith in God! **Are you intimidated to walk in faith for fear that someone will mock you? Have you been mocked before and has that made you faith-shy?**

———

12. **Mark 16:11-18**—When they heard that Jesus was alive and that she had seen him, they did not **believe** it. Afterward Jesus appeared in a different form to two of them while they were walking in the country. These returned and reported it to the rest; but they did not **believe** them either. Later Jesus appeared to the Eleven as they were eating; he rebuked them for their lack of **faith** and their stubborn refusal to **believe** those who had seen him after he had risen. He said to them, "Go

into all the world and preach the good news to all creation. Whoever **believes** and is baptized will be saved, but whoever does not **believe** will be condemned. And these signs will accompany those who **believe**: In my name they will drive out demons; they will speak in new tongues; they will pick up snakes with their hands; and when they drink deadly poison, it will not hurt them at all; they will place their hands on sick people, and they will get well."

• **Are you stubbornly refusing to believe, even though people have brought you reports that Jesus is alive and working? Do you have your own "track record" of how the Lord has met your needs?** I know that the Lord has rebuked me for my lack of faith at times, and He may want to rebuke you. Allow Him to do so and receive it with thanks.

• Anyone who believes must do something—go, preach, be baptized, or heal the sick. **What can you do today because you have faith? This week? This month?**

• **Are there signs following your faith?** This passage has certainly been abused and misused over the years. Many don't believe it was even in the original text but was added later. The bottom line is: Your faith should make a difference in what you are able to do, because if you have faith, God works with and through you. I'm not just talking about faith to do miracles of healing but also miracles of daily life in your family, business, and personal life.

NOTE: You can read my comments on duplicate stories in Mark that I already commented on in Matthew.

1. Mark 11:31-32—They discussed it among themselves and said, "If we say, 'From heaven,' he will ask, 'Then why didn't you **believe** him?' But if we say, 'From men'...." (They feared the people, for everyone held that John really was a prophet.) See number 15 in chapter one, Matthew 21:23-27.

2. Mark 13:21—"At that time if anyone or, 'Look, there he is!' do not **believe** it." See number 17 in chapter one, Matthew 24:23-28.

CONCLUSION

What did you see in Mark's gospel that you didn't notice in Matthew's? What is your action plan now that you have finished another gospel? What answers to my faith questions stand out the most to you? What did you learn?

Once again, I urge you not to hurry on but to linger and learn from God's Word. Remember, the goal of *The Faith Files* is to stimulate faith for daily living, not just to study faith. When I was in high school, I dissected a frog in biology class. At the end of the dissection, I no longer had a frog but all the parts of a frog. We don't want to dissect faith, for then all we will have is faith parts strewn all over our study. Instead, we want living, active faith that makes a difference in people's lives, including our own.

Chapter Three

The Gospel of Luke

My first car was a banana yellow Chevrolet. It was a piece of tin, but it was mine, the first major purchase I had ever made. I loved that car and it served me well. At one point, though, it started falling apart. When I had fixed just about everything there was to fix or replace, I asked the people in my home Bible study group, "I wonder what the Lord is saying about this car?" They gave me an answer that I didn't expect.

One person spoke up and said, "I feel like you are supposed to give that car away." Then a second said, "I was thinking the same thing," It went on like that for the next ten minutes. My wife and I went away from that meeting convinced that God did indeed want us to give our car away. The problem was that it was our only means of transportation.

So I fixed it all up, and we prayed about who the blessed recipient would be. We decided on a family in the church, so we went to the Sunday service with the title and keys in hand. As we told them what we wanted to do, I thought they would break down and cry or give a testimony in church about what we had done. Instead, they said, "That's funny; we had a dream last night that someone gave us a yellow car. Thanks!" And that was it.

At that point, we were without a car, but we determined that we would focus our faith on a new two-tone Ford Granada. We confessed that we had that car, looked out the window every day to see if it was in front of our apartment, and checked the mailbox regularly, expecting to find a check sufficient to cover the new car purchase. Six months later, we were still waiting and frustrated. I decided to go back to my home Bible group for some answers.

"Okay, you guys. You started this," I said. "What am I not seeing here?" Someone then asked me what kind of car we wanted, and I replied that we wanted that two-tone Granada. Someone asked, "What kind of car do you *really* want?" And I gave the same answer. Then a third person asked, "What kind of car do you *really, really* want deep in your heart?"

In anger I responded, "What difference does *that* make? We couldn't afford it anyway." I continued, "What I *really* want is a metallic green Peugeot like I saw the other day with cloth seats, power windows, and the deluxe add-on package."

The group determined that was the car for us and proceeded to give us $2,000 that night toward its purchase. That was the second time I had left a meeting about my car in shock! I didn't want to go to the bank to borrow the money, but I had no choice at that point. We were approved for the loan, and the following Sunday, we drove out of the showroom with our brand-new Peugeot, complete with cloth seats and the deluxe add-on package. (They had opened the dealership on a Sunday especially to sell us that car.)

A week later, a man in our church came to congratulate us on our new car. I told him I wasn't happy that I had to borrow money for the car, and he agreed we should not have done that. So he loaned us the money interest free to pay off the bank, with the stipulation we pay him back as we could. We had the car paid off in two years.

I have drawn on the lessons we learned through this experience many times and have used that story to encourage others as they believed God for provision.

When was your last faith testimony of how God provided for you? When was the last time you told it to someone?

Now let's continue our study of faith in the gospels, looking to Jesus' own words in Luke's gospel.

———————

Luke's gospel is my personal favorite, for he wrote from the perspective of Paul's ministry, since Luke traveled with Paul extensively. This is probably why Luke portrayed so many stories of Jesus working with Gentiles. What's more, Luke is the only Gentile writer in the Bible and wrote his gospel for a Roman audience. Thus, Luke focused on women, the poor, and Jesus—the Man who bore our burdens and sorrows.

Using the NIV version as a reference, I found that Luke used the word *faith* 13 times; *believe, believed,* and *believing* ten times; and *unbelieving* and *unbelief* once each, for a total of twenty-five faith references in this gospel.

1. **Luke 1:19-20**—The angel answered, "I am Gabriel. I stand in the presence of God, and I have been sent to speak to you and to tell you this good news. And now you will be silent and not able to speak until the day this happens, because you did not **believe** my words, which will come true at their proper time."

• I would like to think that if I saw an angel, I would believe what he said. Unbelief is not necessarily eliminated, however, just because someone has a supernatural encounter of some kind. If that were true, then everyone who had seen Jesus' miracles would have turned to God in faith. That did not happen then, nor does it happen today.

• Not having faith limited Zechariah's ability to speak. **Is lack of faith hindering your ability to communicate effectively?** Your doubt may render you ineffective in talking about God and what He is doing and can do for others and for you.

• Zechariah needed a change of heart and mind. He had grown used to their inability to have a child. Contrast him with the blind man in the gospel of Mark who did not grow comfortable with his condition but cried out to God so vehemently that those around him were annoyed. **Are you annoying anyone in your faith pursuit of God? Have you grown accustomed to some subnormal condition in your life? If so, what are you prepared to do about it?**

• Zechariah was a priest. Spiritual authority and position don't guarantee a vibrant faith walk or perspective. **Have you grown sophisticated in your maturity and stopped having faith to believe God for the impossible?**

• God does expect more from those who have known Him longer. When Mary asked a similar question to that of Zechariah's, she received an answer. Zechariah was a priest who was supposed to understand the things of God. When he asked, the angel rendered him mute for nine months.

———————

2. **Luke 1:45**—Blessed is she who has **believed** that what the Lord has said to her will be accomplished.

• Elizabeth declared that Mary was blessed—not because she

was carrying Jesus, but because she had faith! Mary was a young lady, but she believed God for great accomplishments. God spoke to her about matters that had never been heard of before, yet she accepted them with humility and innocent trust. She is a model of faith!

• When Mary asked the angel how it was possible that she was pregnant, Gabriel responded that this was accomplished in the power of the Spirit. I maintain that Mary had no more information than she had before she asked, because Mary did not have a theology of the Spirit as we do today. She just accepted the angel's words that God would do it and asked no more questions.

• How can you imitate Mary's faith? How can you be blessed by believing all that the Lord has promised you?

3. **Luke 5:18-20**—Some men came carrying a paralytic on a mat and tried to take him into the house to lay him before Jesus. When they could not find a way to do this because of the crowd, they went up on the roof and lowered him on his mat through the tiles into the middle of the crowd, right in front of Jesus. When Jesus saw their **faith**, he said, "Friend, your sins are forgiven."

• This account is found in Matthew, Mark, and Luke. Obviously, there is something important about this story that the Holy Spirit wants you to see and comprehend. **Is it the boldness of the friends? Is it their total lack of regard for the house, which could be rebuilt, in favor of their friend, who needed "rebuilt"? Is it Jesus "caught" in the act of forgiving sins, which was controversial to the observers?**

• We don't know anything about the paralytic's faith. He could have been carried against his wishes. **Can you have faith for someone who doesn't?** Perhaps this is no different from when you pray for someone. You "carry" them to God, asking the Lord to do for our friends or family what we cannot do. **Whom are you carrying to God in prayer?**

• These friends certainly were "on the line," so to speak, for they had put their faith out there for everyone to see. If nothing had happened, they would have looked foolish. Instead, they are held up for honor to all gospel readers everywhere for all time. That's the kind of faith legacy I would like to leave. **What kind of faith legacy would you like to have?**

---

4. **Luke 7:3-10**—The centurion heard of Jesus and sent some elders of the Jews to him, asking him to come and heal his servant. When they came to Jesus, they pleaded earnestly with him, "This man deserves to have you do this, because he loves our nation and has built our synagogue." So Jesus went with them. He was not far from the house when the centurion sent friends to say to him: "Lord, don't trouble yourself, for I do not deserve to have you come under my roof. That is why I did not even consider myself worthy to come to you. But say the word, and my servant will be healed. For I myself am a man under authority, with soldiers under me. I tell this one, 'Go,' and he goes; and that one, 'Come,' and he comes. I say to my servant, 'Do this,' and he does it."

When Jesus heard this, he was amazed at him, and turning to the crowd following him, he said, "I tell you, I have not found such great **faith** even in Israel." Then the men who had been sent returned to the house and found the servant well.

• That is another story in the first three gospels. Pay attention to its lessons. There seem to be levels of faith; some have little and some have great faith. This centurion had great faith. **How would you rate your faith level?**

• **Faith the size of a mustard seed can move mountains; what was this centurion capable of doing with great faith?** Jesus healed the servant and didn't ever see or touch him; the power of God was released by the centurion's faith, and Jesus wasn't even present to facilitate the healing.

• **What would happen if you and I had the same level of confident faith that the centurion had?** The centurion was a military man who understood the concept of authority. He knew if Jesus would give the word, then the authority that Jesus had in the spiritual world would do the job. The centurion subtly but accurately acknowledged Jesus' supremacy over the spirit world and disease by what he said about authority. The centurion was acknowledging that Jesus was (and is) God.

• This story shows that someone who isn't a part of your normal circle of fellowship can have great faith in Jesus. (The centurion was not a Jew but had more faith than any Jew had.) You may encounter someone with faith, but they don't talk or think like you, and they may not belong to your "group."

• **Can you make room in your heart for those people? Can you make room in your theology that God is with them, just as He is with you? How can you expand your circle of fellowship to encounter more people like that? What if that**

person isn't as holy or mature as you would expect, yet you still see that they have faith? How will you respond?

———=>●<=———

5. **Luke 7:37-50**—When a woman who had lived a sinful life in that town learned that Jesus was eating at the Pharisee's house, she brought an alabaster jar of perfume, and as she stood behind him at his feet weeping, she began to wet his feet with her tears. Then she wiped them with her hair, kissed them and poured perfume on them. When the Pharisee who had invited him saw this, he said to himself, "If this man were a prophet, he would know who is touching him and what kind of woman she is—that she is a sinner."

Jesus answered him, "Simon, I have something to tell you." "Tell me, teacher," he said. "Two men owed money to a certain moneylender. One owed him five hundred denarii, and the other fifty. Neither of them had the money to pay him back, so he canceled the debts of both. Now which of them will love him more?" Simon replied, "I suppose the one who had the bigger debt canceled." "You have judged correctly," Jesus said.

Then he turned toward the woman and said to Simon, "Do you see this woman? I came into your house. You did not give me any water for my feet, but she wet my feet with her tears and wiped them with her hair. You did not give me a kiss, but this woman, from the time I entered, has not stopped kissing my feet. You did not put oil on my head, but she has poured perfume on my feet. Therefore, I tell you, her many sins have been forgiven—for she loved much. But he who has been forgiven little loves little." Then Jesus said to her, "Your sins are forgiven." The other guests began to say among themselves, "Who is this who even forgives sins?" Jesus said to the woman, "Your **faith** has saved you; go in peace."

• In the previous faith picture, we saw a Roman centurion, who wasn't a Jew, receive a faith miracle. Now Jesus performed a miracle on behalf of a woman. Jewish men were bigoted toward both Gentiles and women, but Jesus demonstrated that God did not share the same prejudices. What's more, this woman was a sinner, yet she pressed through her labels of "woman" and "sinner" to come in faith to Jesus.

• She had faith that, although a sinner, she could approach Jesus and not be rejected, harmed, or rebuked. **Do you? Do you run *to* Him when you've sinned or run *from* Him?**

• Her faith put her in touch with tremendous blessings— peace, forgiveness, and true worship. Yet this whole scene makes me uncomfortable. The woman became very intimate with Jesus when she cleaned His feet. Perhaps prostitution was this woman's sin, so this would make the scene all the more awkward for those watching. I know it is awkward for me, and I'm just reading about it. Jesus refused to let the focus stray but used the opportunity to teach about forgiveness. *Help me, Lord, to be more like Jesus!*

• This is the second case (the other being the paralytic lowered through the roof) in which the Lord forgave sins in response to someone coming to Him in faith.

• People judged this woman and Jesus harshly because of

what she did. Some people don't like it when God responds to the faith of those we have determined to be "unworthy" people. Faith qualifies you and me to receive the blessings of God; it qualifies other people too, even people with whom we are not comfortable.

• It seems that Jesus sent people forth in peace when they came in faith. **If I lack peace, therefore, is that an indication that I lack faith? In what situation do you lack peace today? Is that an indication that you have little faith? What decision can you make today to restore your peace?**

———◦———

6. **Luke 8:10-13**—He said, "The knowledge of the secrets of the kingdom of God has been given to you, but to others I speak in parables, so that, 'though seeing, they may not see; though hearing, they may not understand.' This is the meaning of the parable: The seed is the word of God. Those along the path are the ones who hear, and then the devil comes and takes away the word from their hearts, so that they may not **believe** and be saved. Those on the rock are the ones who receive the word with joy when they hear it, but they have no root. They **believe** for a while, but in the time of testing they fall away."

• Times of testing can cause you to lose your faith, not in God, but in His desire or ability to do something specific that you need or that He promised.

• The forces of darkness work to undermine your faith. Your intellect isn't the only opposition in your life where faith is concerned. Sometimes it is spiritual opposition from God's enemy, who tries to limit your ability to operate in faith.

• All faith will be tested. That means that God seldom follows our timetable for prayer or faith answers. **What are you believing the Lord for today that, if He does not come through, you will look foolish? Can you rejoice that your faith will be tested?**

• The Word of God is the focus for our faith—first for salvation and then for growth and progress in our walk with the Lord. God sets the agenda for our faith. When He opens our eyes to truth, or we come to see a promise, we must respond in faith. This parable shows, however, that it all starts with God, who uses others to sow the seed of His Word in us.

7. **Luke 8:22-25**—One day Jesus said to his disciples, "Let's go over to the other side of the lake." So they got into a boat and set out. As they sailed, he fell asleep. A squall came down on the lake, so that the boat was being swamped, and they were in great danger. The disciples went and woke him, saying, "Master, Master, we're going to drown!" He got up and rebuked the wind and the raging waters; the storm subsided, and all was calm. "Where is your **faith**?" he asked his disciples. In fear and amazement they asked one another, "Who is this? He commands even the winds and the water, and they obey him."

• This story is in all three of the synoptic gospels. **What is it that God wants to make sure we see by repeating it so many times?**

• How tired Jesus must have been to sleep through the storm. Jesus modeled the faith that He expected others to have. He knew that the Father was in control while He slept, so He could sleep well. Even though they were in great danger, He slept soundly. Again, we see that peace is the by-product of faith.

• Jesus initiated this dilemma by suggesting that they set out for the other side of the lake. He expected the disciples to respond in faith to the crisis. They didn't and He rebuked them, along with the wind and rain. **Are you in a crisis right now? Are you responding in faith?** If not, then God may rebuke you too.

———

8. **Luke 8:43-48**—And a woman was there who had been subject to bleeding for twelve years, but no one could heal her. She came up behind him and touched the edge of his cloak, and immediately her bleeding stopped. "Who touched me?" Jesus asked. When they all denied it, Peter said, "Master, the people are crowding and pressing against you." But Jesus said, "Someone touched me; I know that power has gone out from me." Then the woman, seeing that she could not go unnoticed, came trembling and fell at his feet. In the presence of all the people, she told why she had touched him and how she had been instantly healed. Then he said to her, "Daughter, your **faith** has healed you. Go in peace."

• Once again, we read a story that is included in all three gospels. **What is the lesson or lessons that the Lord wants us to see by including this particular story three different times?**

• According to the Law, Jesus was made unclean by having contact with a woman who was bleeding. This story shows, however, that faith goes beyond the law. This encounter rendered neither Jesus nor the woman unclean. **Are you experiencing a situation or encounter with someone whom you fear will make you unclean—such as a homosexual, a person suffering with AIDS or some other disease, or someone from another race or ethnic group?**

• **How could the Law possibly have made anyone "unclean**?" According to the Law, a chance physical encounter, such as brushing up against someone in a crowd, could make someone unclean. To make matters worse, the person made unclean would not even *know* they were unclean because they could not know the condition of the person who touched them. Jesus showed the Jews and us a better way to be clean before God, and that is through faith!

• Up to that point in her life, no one was able to heal her, but her faith in God healed her *instantly*.

• Once again, we see that Jesus sent someone away in peace. God wants you and me to live in peace. **Do you have peace? If not, how can you get it, based on what you have read so far?**

• **Is there some situation in your life where you are putting your faith in everything and everyone except God, as this woman did? If so, can you trust God today and see that longstanding situation resolved?**

---

9. **Luke 8:49-53**—While Jesus was still speaking, someone came from the house of Jairus, the synagogue ruler. "Your daughter is dead," he said. "Don't bother the teacher any more." Hearing this, Jesus said to Jairus,

"Don't be afraid; just **believe**, and she will be healed."
When he arrived at the house of Jairus, he did not let
anyone go in with him except Peter, John and James,
and the child's father and mother. Meanwhile, all the
people were wailing and mourning for her. "Stop
wailing," Jesus said. "She is not dead but asleep." They
laughed at him, knowing that she was dead.

• This is another story that is included in all three gospels.
**What are the lessons we need to learn from this story, since
it is obviously one God doesn't want us to miss?**

• Jesus never saw a dead person, demon, illness, or situation
that intimidated Him. He did not heal or correct every situation,
but we see that He had the power to do so.

• Jesus showed God's compassion for the human conditions
that afflict us. When those conditions continue and God doesn't
intervene, it's not because He isn't compassionate. It's because
He is working something else into our faith. **Is there some situation that you still think about in which God did not act as
you had hoped? Has that situation affected your faith walk?
Are you hesitant to believe again because you were previously disappointed?**

10. **Luke 9:37-41**—The next day, when they came down
from the mountain, a large crowd met him. A man in the
crowd called out, "Teacher, I beg you to look at my son,
for he is my only child. A spirit seizes him and he
suddenly screams; it throws him into convulsions so that
he foams at the mouth. It scarcely ever leaves him and is
destroying him. I begged your disciples to drive it out,

but they could not." "O **unbelieving** and perverse generation," Jesus replied, "how long shall I stay with you and put up with you? Bring your son here."

• It seems that people's lack of faith bothered Jesus. Perhaps by that time they had observed enough that they should have known that Jesus could do anything if people had faith. **How would Jesus feel about your faith level?**

• Notice how Jesus worked to solve practical, everyday life problems. Our faith must focus on the same things. **Where is your faith focus right now? Is it on the same kinds of things on which Jesus focused? How can you improve your faith focus for everyday living?**

• The father had great faith to go past the disciples, who had problems helping his son, to Jesus, whom the father *knew* could help. I know many people who have stopped seeking God because of some disappointment with God's servants. **Has that happened to you?** We shouldn't ever give up on God because of the failures of His people.

---

11. **Luke 12:22-28**—Then Jesus said to his disciples: "Therefore I tell you, do not worry about your life, what you will eat; or about your body, what you will wear. Life is more than food, and the body more than clothes. Consider the ravens: They do not sow or reap, they have no storeroom or barn; yet God feeds them. And how much more valuable you are than birds! Who of you by worrying can add a single hour to his life? Since you cannot do this very little thing, why do you worry about the rest? "Consider how the lilies grow. They do not

labor or spin. Yet I tell you, not even Solomon in all his splendor was dressed like one of these. If that is how God clothes the grass of the field, which is here today, and tomorrow is thrown into the fire, how much more will he clothe you, O you of little **faith**!"

• **Is all worry the result of a lack of faith? What is worry?** I think it is emotional, intellectual, and spiritual preoccupation with matters we cannot change.

• Truth be known, I don't want to live as simply as the ravens; I want more, and that leads to my anxiety to obtain all the stuff I would like to have.

• Ravens don't have relationships, and those certainly complicate our lives and can also be a source of worry. I am also not to worry about other people; they are in God's hands.

• **What other areas of life are worrisome for you? How can you apply this passage to those areas? What can you do to have peace and relax where the issues and necessities of life are concerned?**

---

12. **Luke 17:3-10**—So watch yourselves. "If your brother sins, rebuke him, and if he repents, forgive him. If he sins against you seven times in a day, and seven times comes back to you and says, 'I repent,' forgive him." The apostles said to the Lord, "Increase our **faith**!" He replied, "If you have **faith** as small as a mustard seed, you can say to this mulberry tree, 'Be uprooted and planted in the sea,' and it will obey you. Suppose one of you had a servant plowing or looking after the sheep.

Would he say to the servant when he comes in from the field, 'Come along now and sit down to eat'? Would he not rather say, 'Prepare my supper, get yourself ready and wait on me while I eat and drink; after that you may eat and drink'? Would he thank the servant because he did what he was told to do? So you also, when you have done everything you were told to do, should say, 'We are unworthy servants; we have only done our duty.'"

• Forgiving others is not a matter of faith but a matter of obedience.

• Jesus wanted His followers to know the difference between God's business and our own. Forgiving others is our business; forgiving sins is God's business.

• Jesus did not answer this request to increase their faith because that is not what they needed. They needed to make a decision to forgive; prayer could not help them do that. **Is there anyone you need to forgive? Is there anyone you need to forgive again whom you have already forgiven?** It is a decision, not a feeling.

• Faith is related to God forgiving us; we have seen several instances of someone's faith leading Jesus to pronounce his or her sins forgiven. Our forgiveness of others is a matter of obedience. Jesus' forgiveness of us is pure grace. Yet we still must come to Him in faith.

---

13. **Luke 17:12-19**—As he was going into a village, ten men who had leprosy met him. They stood at a distance and called out in a loud voice, "Jesus, Master, have pity

on us!" When he saw them, he said, "Go, show your-selves to the priests." And as they went, they were cleansed. One of them, when he saw he was healed, came back, praising God in a loud voice. He threw himself at Jesus' feet and thanked him—and he was a Samaritan. Jesus asked, "Were not all ten cleansed? Where are the other nine? Was no one found to return and give praise to God except this foreigner?" Then he said to him, "Rise and go; your **faith** has made you well."

• This Samaritan was traveling with Jews because they were all lepers. Usually, people from the two cultures did not mix. Their uncleanness brought them into some sort of relationship, accomplishing what their religions could not. Your need will connect you with people with whom you may not otherwise have much association. Your faith will do the same.

• The Samaritan wasn't as motivated to go see the priest, since his focus of worship wasn't in Jerusalem or at the temple. (You may want to look at the Samaritan woman at the well in John 4 and her debate with Jesus as to where people should worship.) The Samaritan leper chose to come back to Jesus, while the Jews went their own way.

• His faith brought him back to the source of his healing; the leper's focus was on God, not on himself or on his religious tradition. Therefore, he came back to worship and give thanks. The others did what the Law required them to do and what Jesus had actually told them to do. The others were bound by the Law; this Samaritan was free to respond in faith with thanksgiving.

• Jesus was surprised that anyone came back, especially a Samaritan. **Are you thankful? Do you express your thanks to God on a regular basis? When is the last time you surprised God with your faith?**

———————

14. **Luke 18:1-8**—Then Jesus told his disciples a parable to show them that they should always pray and not give up. He said: "In a certain town there was a judge who neither feared God nor cared about men. And there was a widow in that town who kept coming to him with the plea, 'Grant me justice against my adversary.' For some time he refused. But finally he said to himself, 'Even though I don't fear God or care about men, yet because this widow keeps bothering me, I will see that she gets justice, so that she won't eventually wear me out with her coming!'" And the Lord said, "Listen to what the unjust judge says. And will not God bring about justice for his chosen ones, who cry out to him day and night? Will he keep putting them off? I tell you, he will see that they get justice, and quickly. However, when the Son of Man comes, will he find **faith** on the earth?"

• If you have faith, you will pray.

• When God's answer to our faith petition is delayed, we can become discouraged and stop praying. Jesus urged us in this passage not to let that happen.

• God will answer quickly, but His interpretation and our interpretation of "quickly" are often two very different things.

• **Even though you pray regularly, is there some particular** need for which you have stopped praying, having given up due to a delayed response from God?

• Should people give up on their faith agenda because God responds "slowly"? Have you?

———————

15. **Luke 18:35-43**—As Jesus approached Jericho, a blind man was sitting by the roadside begging. When he heard the crowd going by, he asked what was happening. They told him, "Jesus of Nazareth is passing by." He called out, "Jesus, Son of David, have mercy on me!" Those who led the way rebuked him and told him to be quiet, but he shouted all the more, "Son of David, have mercy on me!" Jesus stopped and ordered the man to be brought to him. When he came near, Jesus asked him, "What do you want me to do for you?" "Lord, I want to see," he replied. Jesus said to him, "Receive your sight; your **faith** has healed you." Immediately he received his sight and followed Jesus, praising God. When all the people saw it, they also praised God.

• It seems obvious what the blind man wanted, but Jesus required him to verbalize his request. Too often, my prayer consists of vague words offered in begging, tentative, and uncertain tones. That is what I call "Godspeak." I have heard people pray and say God's name every third word. I have heard people shout, convinced that the urgency in their tone would increase the chances that God would hear and answer them. That isn't prayer; it's religious babbling and tradition! This man was clear and concise. That is what God requires of you and me. **Are your prayers encumbered with trite or repetitive phrases? Do you raise your voice every time you pray publicly? Is that evidence of faith?**

• This blind man cried out; he didn't pray in Jesus' name. He prayed to Jesus with loud, urgent cries. He wasn't religious. I can understand why a blind man, fearful that Jesus would pass him by, would shout. I can't understand why others do.

• This man did not make peace with his infirmity. He could have gotten accustomed to his limitation. **Have you grown accustomed to some limitation (not just physical) that God wants to reverse? Are you satisfied with less than you could have in faith?**

• **Are you specific enough in your prayer life? Or are you afraid to ask God for something? Why are you afraid? Do you take on religious tones when you pray, especially repeating God's name numerous times in one prayer? Why do you do that?**

• When faith cries are answered, people praise God. Faith answers seldom come without others knowing about it; the answers are intended to encourage everyone and direct their attention to God.

---

16. **Luke 20:1-5**—One day as he was teaching the people in the temple courts and preaching the gospel, the chief priests and the teachers of the law, together with the elders, came up to him. "Tell us by what authority you are doing these things," they said. "Who gave you this authority?" He replied, "I will also ask you a question. Tell me, John's baptism—was it from heaven, or from men?" They discussed it among themselves and said, "If we say, 'From heaven,' he will ask, 'Why didn't you **believe** him?'"

• The Pharisees had developed a system that was the antithesis of faith. They had to do away with Jesus because He was interfering with their system and their understanding of God that they had developed.

• That was also why they did not receive what John the Baptist had to say and do. I would like to believe if I had seen all the miracles Jesus did, I would have abandoned my religious system and followed Him.

• There's no guarantee, however, that this would have happened any more in my life than it did for the Pharisees. I can work to preserve my theological position and thus oppose faith. **Are you doing that in any way, shape, or form? Ask God to help you see if you are. Have you built a framework to understand God so that if He works outside that framework, you cannot see or receive what He is doing?**

⎯⎯⎯⎯

17. **Luke 22:31-34**—"Simon, Simon, Satan has asked to sift you as wheat. But I have prayed for you, Simon, that your **faith** may not fail. And when you have turned back, strengthen your brothers." But he replied, "Lord, I am ready to go with you to prison and to death." Jesus answered, "I tell you, Peter, before the rooster crows today, you will deny three times that you know me."

• It seems that faith cannot fail even when we do. Notice what Jesus was praying for here. He prayed that Peter's faith would not fail after Peter did not measure up to his own expectations and confession. Jesus also prayed that Peter would turn and strengthen others, using his faith that remained after his failure.

• We can and should pray that someone else's faith will not fail. We should pray that our own won't fail as well. **For whom are you praying such a prayer?**

• Jesus knew the plot of the enemy against Simon Peter; He was able to pray effectively because He knew the reality Peter was facing. **Do you see any dangers in which others may be? Are you praying for them?** Faith gives you eyes to see; use them and then pray accordingly.

• Perhaps Peter failed because he overestimated his own spiritual condition. He thought he was able to take a stand that he was not able to make. Paul wrote: "For by the grace given me I say to every one of you: Do not think of yourself more highly than you ought, but rather think of yourself with sober judgment, in accordance with the measure of faith God has given you" (Romans 12:3). **Do you have an accurate assessment of your measure of faith and spiritual state? If not, how can you get this accurate assessment?**

———

18. **Luke 22:67**—"If you are the Christ," they said, "tell us." Jesus answered, "If I tell you, you will not **believe** me."

• Faith leads to miracles, but not all miracles lead to faith. I didn't think of that phrase; Phillip Yancey did. There is a major difference between asking questions to get truth and asking questions to prove what I already believe.

• The Pharisees wanted Jesus to tell them who He was so they could put Him on trial and find Him guilty. They weren't looking for proof that what He was saying was true. They already believed He was a liar and were trying to do away with Him.

• The Pharisees were so set in their thinking that they were no longer pursuing truth but a confirmation of what they already believed. *Lord, help me not to get so hardened that I cannot see You. Also, don't let me get so set in my thinking that I actually oppose You as You work to expand my faith and understanding of Your great love for others and me.* **Can you pray that prayer with me?**

———

19. **Luke 24:9-11**—When they came back from the tomb, they told all these things to the Eleven and to all the others. It was Mary Magdalene, Joanna, Mary the mother of James, and the others with them who told this to the apostles. But they did not **believe** the women, because their words seemed to them like nonsense.

• Faith reports sometimes seem like nonsense.

• Receiving what someone else has experienced and seen can be difficult, but it is foolish not to do so.

• The apostles had no concept of resurrection; therefore, the report did not seem in the realm of possibility. It's difficult to receive a faith report if you don't believe that faith can do what is being reported. If that's the case, even your friends and trusted associates won't be able to convince you! **Has someone been trying to tell you something that God has done for him or her, but you cannot receive it? Ask God to show you where this may be happening.**

———

20. Luke 24:25—He said to them, "How foolish you are, and how slow of heart to **believe** all that the prophets have spoken!"

• Faith is a heart matter. **Is your heart hard or slow to believe?** There is only one way out of a hard heart: faith that gives grace that leads to repentance can change your heart condition.

• **Do you need to repent of being slow to believe? In what area? What difference do you think that will make in your life?**

• Jesus thinks it's foolish *not* to have faith, which means that a fool has no faith. Don't be a fool.

20. Luke 24:41—And while they still did not **believe** it because of joy and amazement, he asked them, "Do you have anything here to eat?"

• Jesus' appearance was too good to be true. Therefore, they could not believe due to their joy and surprise. It was better than anything they could have imagined. **Have you ever been very surprised and said, "I can't believe it"?** We need to learn to say, "That's great! I believe it!"

• God wants to do some I-can't-believe-it miracles for you. You've heard the phrase, "If it's too good to be true, it probably is." That's not the case where faith is concerned. Faith promises and results are the only things in life that are not too good to be true.

• **Can you open yourself to the love of God and His desire to surprise you with His goodness? What in your past keeps you from embracing His desire not just to tolerate you but also to celebrate and bless you?**

CONCLUSION

Go back and review the faith stories that were in all three of the synoptic gospels. There are six of them:

- Jesus calms the storm when awakened—
  Matthew 8:23,27; Mark 4:36-41; Luke 8:22-25.

- Jesus casts out a legion of demons—
  Matthew 8:28-34; Mark 5:1-17; Luke 8:26-37.

- Jesus heals the man who was lowered through the roof by his friends—Matthew 9:1-8; Mark 2:3-12; Luke 5:18-26.

- Jesus raises a dead girl—
  Matthew 9:18,23; Mark 5:31-24, 36-43; Luke 8:49-53.

- On the way to the girl, a bleeding woman is healed—
  Matthew 9:28-36; Mark 5:22-43; Luke 8:41,56.

- A father approached Jesus to heal his son—
  Matthew 17:4-19; Mark 9:14-28; Luke 9:37-42.

• **Why do you think these stories were repeated three times? What does God want us to learn from these stories?**

Chapter Four

The Gospel of John—Part One

In 2003, I was invited to participate in a conference in Afghanistan at Kabul University. The invitation came while I was in Zimbabwe, and I was tired and had no money. I would have to come up with the $5,000 needed to go, and I just didn't have the energy. I would only be home for four weeks before I would have to make the journey to an unstable land where Americans were not so popular.

I always have trouble, however, saying no to an opportunity if money, or lack of it, is the only reason. I feel like I am holding God up with a gun, figuratively of course, and saying, "Give me your money or I won't do what You want." So I left the door open to going but still said, "Not at this time."

About one week later, I met a young woman who had just come back from Kabul and had been the one instrumental in my invitation. She told me that it was safe, and she had enjoyed a wonderful stay as the Lord opened many doors of opportunity for her work as a nurse there. She asked if I was going and, when I told her I was not, she was visibly disappointed. All she said, however, was, "Perhaps you should reconsider." I promised I would. I did and still came to the conclusion that I wasn't going.

Then a week later, I was teaching a seminar for fifteen people at Regent University in Virginia Beach, Virginia. I mentioned that I had an invitation to Kabul University, and one of the fifteen raised her hand and said, "I used to attend Kabul University." I was shocked! Three hundred million people in the United States, and I meet someone from Kabul. She asked if I was going, and when I said I wasn't, she had the same look that the first woman had when I told her. All she said was, "You need to reconsider." I did and still said I wasn't going.

Then my wife attended a seminar sponsored by The World Affairs Council. One of the workshops was on rebuilding nations and featured a speaker who had just returned from Afghanistan. When my wife told him I had an invitation to go there, he said, "Well, I hope he's going." At that point, I decided that God was speaking, and I had to go.

The problem was that I had waited so long and only had two weeks to obtain a second passport, a visa, and the $5,000. Through one miracle after another, I got the documents together and $3,500. On the day my plane took off, I was loading my luggage in the car when the phone rang. It was a friend whom I had not seen in fifteen years, who had heard about my trip. He said, "Ann and I want to give you something toward the trip. Would $1,500 help?" I assured him that it would, and I was off to Kabul with everything that I needed to have a great trip. It was a life-changing experience that I thank God I didn't miss.

Do you know what helped me trust the Lord for that trip? It was my past experiences of learning to trust the Lord for a house, a healing, and a vehicle. While I believe we should exercise faith for provision, I think ultimately our faith must be used to take the gospel to the nations. The objective of *The Faith Files* is simple—increasing your faith for daily living. Is that happening? Remember, you don't need to learn more about faith. You need to apply faith to your daily life and collect faith stories of how God worked on your behalf as you trusted Him.

Now let's continue our study of faith in the gospels, focusing our study on Jesus' own words in the gospel of John.

⟐

There is no agreement today as to whether or not the apostle John wrote this gospel. (Historically, John the apostle is believed to be the author.) It was obviously written long after the other three were compiled. What's more, John's gospel contains a lot of material not included in the other three yet was written by someone who had great familiarity with Jerusalem and its environs. Since there is so much material on faith in John's gospel, I have divided John's study into two sections.

Using the NIV version as a reference, I found that John used the word *faith* nine times; *believe, believing, and believed* ninety-five times; and *trust* once, for a total of one hundred five "**faith**" references in this gospel.

1. **John 1:6-7**—There came a man who was sent from God; his name was John. He came as a witness to testify concerning that light, so that through him all men might **believe**.

• God the Father wants all men to believe and have faith in Him and His Son, Jesus. He sent John for that reason; He may also send you and me to serve other people, to stir up their faith in Him. **Is there any place you are *not* willing to go for God? Where is it? Why won't you go? What are you afraid of?**

• We can only bear witness to what we know and have seen God do. God has put you through some of the things you have gone through to bear witness to His light and grace in times of trouble so that others may believe.

68

• You don't have to fully explain or theologically understand what God has done for you. You just have to be a witness to the truth! **What truth can you testify of and be certain that you know?**

————❖————

2. **John 1:12-13**—Yet to all who received him, to those who **believed** in his name, he gave the right to become children of God—children born not of natural descent, nor of human decision or a husband's will, but born of God.

• Faith makes you part of God's family. Whether your natural family wanted or planned to have you, faith gives you rights—rights as a child of God.

• Not all men and women are God's children, but only those who put their faith in Jesus! We are not all brothers and sisters just because we are human. We are only brothers and sisters when we have the same Father, and faith brings us into relationship with our Father through Jesus. There is no such thing as the brotherhood of man—only the brotherhood of the believers. **Does this make sense to you? What does it say to other groups who want us all to embrace our "brotherhood" apart from God the Father?**

————❖————

3. **John 1:50-51**—Jesus said, "You **believe** because I told you I saw you under the fig tree. You shall see greater things than that." He then added, "I tell you the truth, you shall see heaven open, and the angels of God ascending and descending on the Son of Man."

• This man Nathaniel heard something that he knew could only have come from God. That gave him faith. God is not against showing you miracles upon which you can base your trust in Him. Ultimately, however, your faith must be in God and not in what God does. **Is that where you have placed your trust?**

• Sometimes faith requires understanding a riddle or a truth that is a bit shrouded from sight. Jesus here was referring to the dream that Isaac had, as described in Genesis 28:12. When that happens, you need to have faith that you will eventually see and understand. This is what I call "faith tension." Your mind struggles to grasp the meaning, but your will says, "Hold on, mind. The answer isn't clear now, but it will come to us." That's operating in healthy faith tension.

———————

4. **John 2:11**—This, the first of his miraculous signs, Jesus performed at Cana in Galilee. He thus revealed His glory, and His disciples put their **faith** in Him.

• **Isn't turning water into wine at a wedding feast an interesting way for Jesus to start His public miracle ministry?** The water was held in large jars that were in the house for ceremonial washing. It seems to me that Jesus was responding to Mary's faith, even though He was reluctant to do so. **Was it just because she was His mother?** I don't think so. I think God responds to faith no matter who has it. Faith plays no favorites with God! He responded to a Roman centurion, a synagogue ruler, His mother, and the Shunnamite woman when they had faith. He will respond to you as well.

• Faith takes you from the realm of the Law and predictability to the realm of grace and unpredictability. This miracle symbolized a new order with new rules of how to relate to God the Creator. This miracle was symbolic in that what had been used as a common source of cleansing (the Law) would now be turned into a source of joy and grace in the person of Jesus.

• Faith produces miracles. We have established that in this case Jesus responded to Mary's faith. She told the attendants to do whatever He directed them to do. **How did she know He would say anything?** Based on His initial response, it didn't seem like He would do or say anything. She believed, and her faith saved the wedding hosts from an embarrassing moment. It doesn't seem like the hosts knew what was going on. **How are you applying your faith to change situations? Do people and situations improve when you show up? Are you willing to change things for the better and not have people know what you did?**

• This miracle involved speeding up the process of turning water to wine, which is usually a more natural, slower production process (water to vines to grapes to juice to wine). **Which other of Jesus' miracles involved a "speeding up" of a natural process like this? How about the cursing of the fig tree that was withered the next day? Can you think of any others?**

• Jesus revealed His glory, and the disciples put their faith in Him. All people are looking to put their faith somewhere: in science, gods, religious systems, the government, economic principles, or other people. Disciples of Jesus are so called because they place their faith in Jesus. **In whom or what are you putting your faith?**

5. **John 2:22-23**—After he was raised from the dead, his disciples recalled what he had said. Then they **believed** the Scripture and the words that Jesus had spoken. Now while he was in Jerusalem at the Passover Feast, many people saw the miraculous signs he was doing and **believed** in his name.

• Faith is a growth process. The disciples had faith after Jesus' resurrection when they were reminded of what Jesus had said. They needed some experience to go along with the Word. **Have you grown in faith?** You probably have. Just consider something that has happened to you lately. **How would you have responded to that challenge five or 10 years ago?** If you responded better today, that's because you have grown in faith. Thank God and congratulations!

• There was the faith of the *casual* follower who saw what Jesus did, but then there was the faith of the *serious* disciple, who struggled with what He said and with the tough issues in the Bible, but who endured to the end, having faith all along. **Into which category do you fit: casual or serious, faith from a distance or faith up close and personal?**

6. **John 3:12**—"I have spoken to you of earthly things and you do not **believe**; how then will you **believe** if I speak of heavenly things?"

• **Does this mean that if we trust God when He speaks to us of earthly things, He will then speak to us of the things of heaven? Is this the order of progression for revelation and insight? Is it fair to say that receiving in and through faith enables you to receive more?**

• It is hard to imagine that someone would *not* believe when God speaks, but it happens. People did not believe what Jesus said then, and some don't believe what He says now. Make sure that isn't happening where you are concerned.

• I think of what it says in Hebrews at this point:

> In fact, though by this time you ought to be teachers, you need someone to teach you the elementary truths of God's word all over again. You need milk, not solid food! Anyone who lives on milk, being still an infant, is not acquainted with the teaching about righteousness. But solid food is for the mature, who by constant use have trained themselves to distinguish good from evil (Hebrews 5:12-14).

• **Are you working toward understanding the things of heaven, or are you still stuck in dealing only with earthly things, according to Jesus' terminology in this verse? Where is this happening in your life?**

———————

7. **John 3:16-18**—"For God so loved the world that he gave his one and only Son, that whoever **believes** in him shall not perish but have eternal life. For God did not send his Son into the world to condemn the world, but to save the world through him. Whoever **believes** in him is not condemned, but whoever does not **believe** stands condemned already because he has not **believed** in the name of God's one and only Son.

• God doesn't condemn people to their current state; their lack of faith takes care of that. Not believing in the name of Jesus has consequences just like jumping off a building. If you jump, you can't curse gravity for taking you down. If you don't believe, you can't curse the condemnation that comes with that. It's a fixed principle. God has provided the way to Him; you can accept or reject it, but you can't change it.

• I believe in the name of Jesus; it's better than the good name of any business or service. If His name is behind anything, it is true, just, and holy.

• Believing that Jesus was a real historical figure isn't enough to satisfy God. You can find Jews today who believe that Jesus existed, just as they believe Napoleon, Charlemagne, or King Henry VIII existed. They have never seen those men of history, but they believe the accounts of their existence. God wants more than that. He wants men and women everywhere to put their faith in the love of God, the words that He has spoken, and His power to grant them eternal life.

• **Is your belief an intellectual one, or a belief that directs your decisions and actions on a daily basis?** That is what God wants, not just a casual faith that Jesus was a good man who walked the earth doing nice things for people.

————————

8. **John 3:36**—Whoever **believes** in the Son has eternal life, but whoever rejects the Son will not see life, for God's wrath remains on him.

• Eternal life is a quality of life so good nothing can stop it! That is the definition a seminary professor gave me. **Do you think it's accurate?**

• Faith leads to eternal life; lack of faith leads to eternal death and God's wrath. **Pretty simple formula, don't you think?**

• Jesus was angered when people lacked faith.

• We are all creatures of faith. We trust that the can of beans for dinner isn't poisoned, that other drivers will stay on their side of the road, that no one will steal our car when we park it at the mall, and that the bridge won't collapse when we drive over it.

• **So why not trust God with childlike faith for what He has promised, especially eternal life?** A life of faith really isn't that strange. In fact, it's normal and a necessary part of our human, earthly experience.

———

9. John 4:21—Jesus declared, "**Believe** me, woman, a time is coming when you will worship the Father neither on this mountain nor in Jerusalem."

• Jesus was exhorting this woman to put her faith in what He was saying. Jesus was prophesying the end of the debate that separated Jews and Samaritans as to the appropriate place to worship God. Faith is not tied to a place but to a person. **Do you believe that? Then why do you call a church building a "house of God?"** I thought the worship of God isn't tied to a place.

• Jesus was encouraging this woman, who had been married to five different men, to have faith in what He said. This shows that anyone can please God through faith, even those with a poor moral past. Oscar Wilde once said, "Every saint has a past;

every sinner has a future." **Does this offend you?** It certainly offended the Jews of Jesus' day, who connected righteousness not to faith but to right living and adherence to the Law.

• Faith is a relationship with God, not a religious system. You can be systematic and consistent in your faith, however, and follow a pattern of trusting Him in any situation. For example, you can be generous at all times, whether you have abundance or lack. That is what I am referring to as systematic faith. That faith isn't based on the circumstances or how you feel or what you have; it's based on a decision to trust God for your own provision as you help others with theirs. **Which do you have— a religious system or a faith system?** Don't answer too quickly until you have reflected on the answer.

---

10. **John 4:39-41**—Many of the Samaritans from that town **believed** in him because of the woman's testimony, "He told me everything I ever did." So when the Samaritans came to him, they urged him to stay with them, and he stayed two days. And because of his words many more became **believers**.

• That woman must have been something! She had five husbands and was then living with another man. Yet she had enough credibility among those with whom she lived that they followed her to Jesus. Or perhaps they just wanted to see any man who could tell "everything" this woman had ever done. They all knew she had done a lot!

• Jesus was a good speaker and teacher (see Mark 12:35-37). People regularly believed, coming to faith because of what He said (see Romans 10:17). Faith comes by hearing and hearing by the Word of God! So if you want your faith to increase, you must be hearing new things. **Does that make sense? What or who are you listening to that has the power to increase your faith?**

• You sometimes need to hear others talking about their faith to bolster your own, since it is God speaking to you through them. **To whom do you listen that builds your faith?**

• Hearing the wrong things, or nothing at all, will weaken or destroy your faith over time.

11. **John 4:42**—They said to the woman, "We no longer **believe** just because of what you said; now we have heard for ourselves, and we know that this man really is the Savior of the world."

• It is possible to have faith in God because of what someone else tells you about Him. Eventually, however, you must find and build your own faith. **Whose faith are you living on right now? Your parents' faith? Your spouse's? Or your own?**

• They had faith because of what they heard. This is why we must magnify God. We must take the smallest thing He has done and "blow it up" so that people can see it more easily. When they see it, it will encourage and increase their faith. **Are you "magnifying the Lord"? What more can you do to broadcast the good things that God has done for you so that others may be encouraged?**

12. John 4:48-53—"Unless you people see miraculous signs and wonders," Jesus told him, "you will never **believe**." The royal official said, "Sir, come down before my child dies." Jesus replied, "You may go. Your son will live." The man took Jesus at his word and departed. While he was still on the way, his servants met him with the news that his boy was living. When he inquired as to the time when his son got better, they said to him, "The fever left him yesterday at the seventh hour." Then the father realized that this was the exact time at which Jesus had said to him, "Your son will live." So he and all his household **believed**.

• **What did the father and his household believe?** They believed that Jesus was who He claimed to be: the Son of God.

• Miracles don't guarantee faith, but faith does guarantee miracles. Think about that statement. **Is it true? Does it make sense?**

• The man left Jesus' presence to go home because He had faith in Jesus' word. He wanted Jesus to come down to where he lived, but what Jesus spoke was good enough for him. What Jesus speaks should be enough for you too. **What promises has God already made to you that you may not be living up to?**

• The man made careful inquiry as to the time of the healing so that he could substantiate the results of his faith. Facts and faith eventually go hand in hand, although for a time they may seem to be at odds. Don't ever think that you must deny the facts to walk in faith. At times, though, you must wait for the facts to catch up with your faith vision.

• Jesus knew that miracles were related to people's ability to believe in who He was and what He could do. Your faith focus cannot be faith; your focus must be God. **Do you think it is possible to have faith in faith instead of faith in God?**

———⇒●⇐———

13. **John 5:24**—I tell you the truth, whoever hears my word and **believes** him who sent me has eternal life and will not be condemned; he has crossed over from death to life.

• **If you have eternal life, why are you worried about this life, which isn't eternal?** This will pass away, but I'm carrying a life in me that will never pass away. That certainly puts things into perspective.

• There is *no* condemnation in Jesus. If you don't say "hallelujah" here, you don't understand what Jesus was (and is) saying. You have access to God for all eternity because of your faith! You and I have already crossed over from death to life (see Romans 8:1).

———⇒●⇐———

14. **John 5:37-47**—And the Father who sent me has himself testified concerning me. You have never heard his voice nor seen his form, nor does his word dwell in you, for you do not **believe** the one he sent. You diligently study the Scriptures because you think that by them you possess eternal life. These are the Scriptures that testify about me, yet you refuse to come to me to have life. I do not accept praise from men, but I know you. I know that you do not have the love of God in your hearts. I have come in my Father's name, and you do not accept me;

but if someone else comes in his own name, you will accept him. How can you **believe** if you accept praise from one another, yet make no effort to obtain the praise that comes from the only God? But do not think I will accuse you before the Father. Your accuser is Moses, on whom your hopes are set. If you **believed** Moses, you would **believe** me, for he wrote about me. But since you do not **believe** what he wrote, how are you going to **believe** what I say?

• Jesus was telling Moses' followers that they didn't believe Moses. How ironic! That means that followers of Jesus may not believe Him either, although they believe that He existed and was raised from the dead. They just don't take His words seriously and apply them to daily living.

• Jesus also told them that Moses was going to accuse them at the judgment because Moses spoke about Jesus! I will eventually write *The Faith Files: Old Testament.* Faith is not exclusively a New Testament concept. Faith has always been the way to God, but the Jews tried to substitute the Law for faith.

• Moses and the Scriptures still talk about having faith in Jesus. Jesus is the goal of your faith. Worship, faith itself, the faith preacher, and Bible knowledge are not your goals. Jesus is!

• You and I must make an effort to obtain the praise that only comes from God. The writer of Hebrews tells us that "without faith it is impossible to please him [God]" (Hebrews 11:6). Men may not praise you if you seek after the Father through Jesus, but God will praise you. In the end, that is all that truly matters. **Whose praise are you seeking?** Faith sometimes causes you to follow God while those closest to you misunderstand. **Are you being misunderstood for your faith?**

15. John 6:29-36—Jesus answered, "The work of God is this: to **believe** in the one he has sent." So they asked him, "What miraculous sign then will you give that we may see it and **believe** you? What will you do? Our forefathers ate the manna in the desert; as it is written: 'He gave them bread from heaven to eat.'" Jesus said to them, "I tell you the truth, it is not Moses who has given you the bread from heaven, but it is my Father who gives you the true bread from heaven. For the bread of God is he who comes down from heaven and gives life to the world." "Sir," they said, "from now on give us this bread." Then Jesus declared, "I am the bread of life. He who comes to me will never go hungry, and he who **believes** in me will never be thirsty. But as I told you, you have seen me and still you do not **believe**."

• Serving Jesus is not based on works but faith. It all starts by believing that He is the one whom God sent. After that, Jesus will give you work to do, but it all starts with faith. You will then also fulfill the good works that God has prepared for you in faith.

• They wanted proof, but Jesus seldom gave His challengers proof on demand. Instead, He actually put up stumbling blocks to make it even harder for them to leave their religious systems and follow Him in faith.

• It is not up to God to adapt to my faith level; it is up to me to adapt to God's faith expectations.

• Tradition said that when the Messiah came, He would give bread to the masses. That is what the people were asking for. They misunderstood what God meant, however, and couldn't see that the bread was going to be a man—Jesus.

• They thought that Moses had given them bread (the desert manna), and the Messiah would do the same. They missed the fact that God the Father gave and would give the Bread of Life, who is Jesus. Your faith focus must be on God and not on what He can bring you or do for you! The people were looking for bread when the Bread of Life walked in their midst.

• **Have you ever misunderstood anything that the Lord was communicating to you? Even now, are you expecting God to act in a certain way, but He comes in another that you don't expect or can't even imagine?** You must stay open to God and not try to figure out His ways.

• Jacob was face-to-face with God in Genesis 26 and didn't know it. **Are you face-to-face with Him in some life situation and don't know it?** You may be and don't recognize what He is doing in your life. Ask Him to show you if that is the case.

16. **John 6:35-47**—Then Jesus declared, "I am the bread of life. He who comes to me will never go hungry, and he who **believes** in me will never be thirsty. But as I told you, you have seen me and still you do not **believe**. All that the Father gives me will come to me, and whoever comes to me I will never drive away. For I have come down from heaven not to do my will but to do the will of him who sent me. And this is the will of him who sent me, that I shall lose none of all that he has given me, but raise them up at the last day. For my Father's will is that everyone who looks to the Son and **believes** in him shall have eternal life, and I will raise him up at the last day."

At this the Jews began to grumble about him because he said, "I am the bread that came down from heaven." They said, "Is this not Jesus, the son of Joseph, whose father and mother we know? How can he now say, 'I came down from heaven'?" "Stop grumbling among yourselves," Jesus answered. "No one can come to me unless the Father who sent me draws him, and I will raise him up at the last day. It is written in the Prophets: 'They will all be taught by God.' Everyone who listens to the Father and learns from him comes to me. No one has seen the Father except the one who is from God; only he has seen the Father. I tell you the truth, he who **believes** has everlasting life."

• If you don't understand the connection between faith and eternal life, you aren't paying attention! Eternal life is a gift, and faith is the voucher that you use to obtain it.

• Jesus repeats this over and over again. Remember, He was saying this to a people who were steeped in a life of religious deeds and good works. This was a radical concept for them, and it is for us too. It just seems too good to be true; there must be something we have to do to earn it, or so many people think.

• There is something in us that wants to earn our blessings from God. Faith, however, is all that is required. **Are you trying to earn God's blessings in any area of your life?** You need to do the work that God has assigned you, but your work can never earn those blessings. **Is that confusing?**

• Anyone that comes to God through faith still can't take credit, for the Father first drew that person to Himself. It all starts and ends with God; Jesus is the author and finisher of our faith (see Hebrews 12:1-2).

17. John 6:64-69—"Yet there are some of you who do not **believe**." For Jesus had known from the beginning which of them did not **believe** and who would betray him. He went on to say, "This is why I told you that no one can come to me unless the Father has enabled him." From this time many of his disciples turned back and no longer followed him. "You do not want to leave too, do you?" Jesus asked the Twelve. Simon Peter answered him, "Lord, to whom shall we go? You have the words of eternal life. We **believe** and know that you are the Holy One of God."

• Judas betrayed Jesus because Judas did not believe that Jesus was God's Son. **Who did he think Jesus was (and is)?** Judas saw Jesus firsthand and yet had no faith! If that can happen to someone who traveled with Jesus daily, it can be true today of someone who has been around the Church and God's people for years.

• Faith is the great enabler, for it enables you to do business with God in God's way. Faith is the currency with which we make transactions with God. It is the means by which anyone can come to the Father through Jesus.

• When Peter asked, "To whom shall we go," it sounds like he had considered his options and concluded that he had none. The disciples thought about leaving but decided against it. That didn't disqualify them as disciples. Faith is difficult sometimes, and God does things that test your ability to go on when you are in pain or confused. If Jesus tested His disciples then, He will do it to us now.

18. John 7:5—For even his own brothers did not **believe** in him.

• Jesus' brothers, those who knew Him best, did not have faith. That must have been painful for Him. Jesus knows what it is like to serve God wholeheartedly and not have your family understand.

• Jesus' brothers were Jews, but their Jewish heritage blinded them to who Jesus truly was.

• This just proves to me that being around the things of God doesn't indicate that you have faith. You can grow up in church but not really know the Lord of the Church. **Do you know about God, or do you know God? Do you know about faith, or have you put your faith and trust in Him for salvation and forgiveness of sins?**

———

19. John 7:27-31—"But we know where this man is from; when the Christ comes, no one will know where he is from." Then Jesus, still teaching in the temple courts, cried out, "Yes, you know me, and you know where I am from. I am not here on my own, but he who sent me is true. You do not know him, but I know him because I am from him and he sent me." At this they tried to seize him, but no one laid a hand on him, because his time had not yet come. Still, many in the crowd put their **faith** in him. They said, "When the Christ comes, will he do more miraculous signs than this man?"

• At times, Jesus did not make it easy to put faith in Him. There were times when He said strange things. He didn't always answer people's questions, and when He did, we can only understand what He meant because we have 2,000 years of history to look back and do so. At that time, they had no idea as to what He was referring. Faith isn't always an easy or clear path to walk.

• Jesus did not quite fit their system or expectations of what the Messiah would be and do. He did things that surprised and even upset them. **Has God done that with you? Has He ever not fit into what you expected Him to be or do?** That is where faith comes in.

• The second commandment forbids any idol worship or strange gods. I have had a strange mental image of God at times, however, and worshiped God as I want Him to be or thought He should be, and not as He truly is. That is an idol as much as any graven image. **Do you have any expectations or images of God that you need to adjust to the reality of who He really is?**

• I must worship God as He is and not as I want Him to be. If I put my faith in Him, I trust that whatever He does is consistent with His loving, holy nature, whether or not I like or understand it. God often disguises Himself and makes it hard to recognize Him using anything but the eyes of faith.

20. **John 7:38-39**—"Whoever **believes** in me, as the Scripture has said, streams of living water will flow from within him." By this he meant the Spirit, whom those who **believed** in him were later to receive. Up to that time the Spirit had not been given, since Jesus had not yet been glorified.

• Not only do we receive eternal life, but we also receive the Spirit as a down payment on that promise of life forevermore.

• Faith causes streams of water to flow out of us, water that others can drink. Your faith refreshes others. **What is it exactly that flows out of us as water?** I think it's words, facial expressions, attitudes, and deeds, to name a few. It's the essence of who you are—your purpose.

• The water that flows, while it comes from God, will taste like you and me. It will sound like us and come from our experience using the gifts that God has given us to express what we see. That's why we have to stay away from bitterness; it gives our water a bad taste. Also, we need to stay away from evil talk; it makes our water salty and unfit to drink (see James 3:9-12). Other than that, that which comes out of us will taste like us.

• The gospel writers were inspired by God when they wrote, yet they used their vocabulary and experience to communicate God's truth. That is an excellent example of what I am saying: the water (in this case, the words) that flowed from them were a river from God that tasted like Matthew, Mark, Luke, and John.

• Faith in Jesus is a prerequisite to receive any measure of the Holy Spirit. Your faith in Jesus will lead you to greater things in God. He rewards those who diligently seek Him (see Hebrews 11:6), and one of the rewards is the Spirit. The word *diligently* can imply a long, arduous process. My definition of what diligent means and Jesus' definition can be very different. My timetable can be very different than God's as well. I think I have been diligent after two weeks, but God may want me to seek Him for two months before He rewards me. **Are you impatient with God's timetable of rewards for you? Are you frustrated or angered over how long you have had to seek Him?**

21. John 7:48—"Has any of the rulers or of the Pharisees **believed** in him?"

• It doesn't matter who does or doesn't believe. It only matters if *you* believe. Don't be influenced by the unbelief of significant or famous people, even spiritual leaders. You must have your own faith, even if you stand alone. For example, many people in the media question God and His Word. Don't be swayed by them no matter how intelligent or famous they may be.

———

22. John 8:24—"I told you that you would die in your sins; if you do not **believe** that I am [the one I claim to be], you will indeed die in your sins."

• Faith, forgiveness of sins, eternal life, and death are all interconnected.

• The Jews had a perfect system, instituted by God, for the forgiveness of sins, or so they thought. Their system, however, was limited. Jesus came to institute faith, but many preferred their system to God's grace. You must be careful not to fall into the same trap today. **Have you put your faith in a system about God or in God Himself?**

———

23. John 8:28-32—So Jesus said, "When you have lifted up the Son of Man, then you will know that I am [the one I claim to be] and that I do nothing on my own but speak just what the Father has taught me. The one who sent me is with me; he has not left me alone, for I always do what pleases him." Even as he spoke, many put their

faith in him. To the Jews who had **believed** him, Jesus said, "If you hold to my teaching, you are really my disciples. Then you will know the truth, and the truth will set you free."

• "They put their faith in him." Almost every day I put my faith in some company's name. I trust that company's claims and products. It is a conscious, rational decision to do so. When I open a can of corn, I have faith that it is healthy to eat. When a company produces a good "name," and I buy something based on that name, it is a great marketing strategy. When I drive, I have faith that the other drivers will stay on their side of the road. **Can you think of other examples of this kind of practical day-to-day faith?** My point is that faith is natural for us; we cannot make it through one day without it.

• It is the same with Jesus. I put my trust in Him and His name. I believe and trust what He says because He has proven Himself to be trustworthy. If His name is connected to anything, it has credibility. You see, faith isn't so strange or exotic after all. You cannot live without faith on a daily basis, whether it's faith in the contents of a can of corn or God's Word. Don't trivialize your faith yearnings, however, by placing them in anything less than Jesus, the Son of God.

• Because I have believed in Him and I have become His follower, He will lead me to the truth—truth that will set me free. Faith frees me from trying to be something I'm not or from figuring everything out before I act. Faith makes me like a child in the Kingdom, and that sets me free!

• **If you aren't free in any area, is it a lack of faith? Lack of obedience to Jesus' teaching? What price are you willing to pay to be free?**

24. John 8:31-36—To the Jews who had **believed** him, Jesus said, "If you hold to my teaching, you are really my disciples. Then you will know the truth, and the truth will set you free." They answered him, "We are Abraham's descendants and have never been slaves of anyone. How can you say that we shall be set free?" Jesus replied, "I tell you the truth, everyone who sins is a slave to sin. Now a slave has no permanent place in the family, but a son belongs to it forever. So if the Son sets you free, you will be free indeed."

• Faith is liberating. It sets us free from having to figure out how to please God. All we have to do is hear, trust, and obey.

- • Faith sets you free to be part of God's family.
- • Faith sets you free from sin.
- • Faith sets you free from limitations.
- • Faith sets you free from wrong doctrines and "faiths."
- • Faith sets you free so that you can know and then do God's will.
- • Faith sets you free to enjoy the gift of eternal life.

• Finish the list. **What else does faith set you free from or for?**

———›•‹———

25. John 8:45-46—"Yet because I tell the truth, you do not **believe** me! Can any of you prove me guilty of sin? If I am telling the truth, why don't you **believe** me?"

• Truth obviously wasn't enough to cause some men to believe Jesus. Those men had an agenda that did not include seeking the truth. They had something to protect—their lifestyle, position, wealth and ethnicity—and were willing to kill Jesus in order to hold onto those things.

• **Have you surrendered all for Jesus? Are you willing to believe Him, even if there is personal cost for you? Can you prove God guilty of something that would justify not putting faith in Him and His Word?**

CONCLUSION

John has more faith references than the other gospel writers combined. This qualifies John to be the faith champion of the gospels! The other three gospels were written before John, and John was probably familiar with their accounts. He had a chance to emphasize anything that he felt was lacking or missing, and thus he chose, with the Spirit's leading, to focus his gospel account on faith. That tells us what John felt was most important—having faith in Jesus, the Son of God.

If that was John's conclusion, shouldn't it be yours as well? When all is said and done, faith, hope, and love will abide forever, as Paul wrote in 1 Corinthians 13:13. Don't ignore or neglect your faith action decisions that you make as you move through *The Faith Files*.

Chapter Five

The Gospel of John—Part Two

In chapter one, I told the story of our house that we purchased through a series of faith actions. We were in that house for five years and enjoyed every day of it. We hosted weddings in our large family room. We had dinner parties and invited family and friends over regularly for cookouts and celebrations. Family came to visit, and my wife's sister lived with us for three years. I had my office in the downstairs bedroom. If ever there was a house we loved, that was the one.

After living there for five years, however, we sensed that God was calling us to pastor a church in Orlando, Florida. That meant we would have to put our beloved house in Mobile, Alabama, on the market. The Orlando church needed someone right away, so we put the house on the market and moved into a rental home in Orlando, 500 miles away. We didn't want a house to hold us in an area when God wanted us to be someplace else. Plus, we just knew that our house would sell quickly because we were doing God's will.

We enjoyed being in Orlando, but the Mobile house didn't sell right away. Truth be told, we were in a rental house for two years while we waited for that house to sell. We prayed, lowered the price, had people walk around the house and declare it sold, prayed some more and struggled every month to make two payments—our rent and our mortgage.

Then one day my children came running into my office with a registered letter. Unbeknownst to me, they had entered my name in a drawing for a free house, and the letter was from the builder and the NBA Orlando Magic, co-sponsors of the house giveaway. We were all so excited. When I opened the letter, I was informed that I was one of fifty finalists. I had to attend a Magic game, shoot one foul shot, and—if I made the shot—my name would be entered in the final drawing. There was no telling how many others would make their shot, so my chances were at worst one in fifty, if I made the shot.

When I looked at the ticket for my game, my heart sank. It was for a Monday night game, and I was scheduled to be away at a church conference. I was the conference coordinator, so there was no way I could not be present. I called the Magic and asked if I could switch games with someone else. They said no. We were all disappointed, but I gave my ticket away and drove to Atlanta the same day that my "shot" at a house had been scheduled.

Needless to say, I was discouraged during the seven-hour drive to Atlanta. "God," I said, "I've done everything I knew to do to sell the house. I moved to Orlando because You wanted me to." Then I continued, "And now I feel like you dangled this house in front of me and jerked it away."

As I drove, I realized that I could view this scenario in one of two ways. I could be discouraged and even angry over what had transpired, or I could see this as a sign from God. God could give me a house when He was ready to do so. I didn't need the Orlando Magic or anyone else to help me. If God was for me—and He was—who could be against me? By the time I arrived in Atlanta, I had made my choice to trust God.

After a two-year wait, we sold the house while I was at that conference! What's more, six months later God miraculously provided, and we bought a house in Orlando complete with a swimming pool. We loved that home too, not because it was the greatest house in the world, but because of what we learned in the process.

Faith doesn't make God your butler who is ready to meet your every wish or need. It doesn't put God at your beck and call. It does, however, give you the means to live every day with confidence and joy. My experience made what Job said a little more real to me:

Naked I came from my mother's womb, and naked I shall return there. The Lord gave and the Lord has taken away. Blessed be the name of the Lord (Job 1:21 NAS)

Though he slay me, yet will I trust in him: but I will maintain mine own ways before him (Job 13:15 KJV).

Now let's return to our study of faith in John's gospel, part two.

———⟫⦁⟪———

There is no special reason why I divided the faith study on John's gospel into two chapters. There were so many references that I thought it would make your study simpler and easier to read by doing so. Keep in mind that this is not a technical study of faith, but a practical study with a view to daily application. It doesn't matter what order you study the references; it's just important that you study them and try to answer the questions that are included. I hope that you are keeping a faith journal to record both what you are learning and new questions you are asking to stimulate and focus your faith walk. So now let's continue our look at what John's gospel has to say about faith.

1. **John 9:18**—The Jews still did not **believe** that he had been blind and had received his sight until they sent for the man's parents.

• Doubt can cause you to reject someone else's report of the truth. This man was born blind, could now see, but the Jews were trying hard to repudiate the man's story.

• Some people in Jesus' day put more faith in being a Jew than they did in knowing God. They put more faith in being a son of Abraham than they placed in the God of Abraham. There are some people like that today. **Do you know any? Are you one of them?** (I hope not.)

• On the one hand, I would rather err on the side of faith than doubt. On the other hand, I want to grow in faith so I can recognize the false while holding on to the true. I don't want to reject a real $20 bill because it may be a counterfeit. I want to recognize the counterfeit so I can enjoy the real thing! I want to live in real faith.

———

2. **John 9:35-38**—Jesus heard that they had thrown him out, and when he found him, he said, "Do you **believe** in the Son of Man?" "Who is he, sir?" the man asked. "Tell me so that I may **believe** in him." Jesus said, "You have now seen him; in fact, he is the one speaking with you." Then the man said, "Lord, I **believe**," and he worshiped him.

• Faith and worship are related in this passage. **Is it accurate to say that you will worship what you put your faith in?**

• Jesus revealed who He was to this man in no uncertain terms, something He rarely did. This man's faith was so great that it caused him to dispute the authorities who had put him out of the synagogue. Jesus then sought out the man to reveal Himself. God does reward those who seek Him (see Hebrews 11:6).

---

3. **John 10:25-39**—Jesus answered, "I did tell you, but you do not **believe**. The miracles I do in my Father's name speak for me, but you do not **believe** because you are not my sheep. My sheep listen to my voice; I know them, and they follow me. I give them eternal life, and they shall never perish; no one can snatch them out of my hand. My Father, who has given them to me, is greater than all; no one can snatch them out of my Father's hand. I and the Father are one."

Again the Jews picked up stones to stone him, but Jesus said to them, "I have shown you many great miracles from the Father. For which of these do you stone me?" "We are not stoning you for any of these," replied the Jews, "but for blasphemy, because you, a mere man, claim to be God." Jesus answered them, "Is it not written in your Law, 'I have said you are gods'? If he called them 'gods,' to whom the word of God came—and the Scripture cannot be broken—what about the one whom the Father set apart as his very own and sent into the world? Why then do you accuse me of blasphemy because I said, 'I am God's Son'?

Do not **believe** me unless I do what my Father does. But if I do it, even though you do not **believe** me, **believe** the miracles, that you may know and understand that the

Father is in me, and I in the Father." Again they tried to seize him, but he escaped their grasp.

• Is faith a gift? Or is faith a decision? Can a person press through a hard heart and intellectualism and come to the knowledge of God without God's help?

• Jesus was urging the Jews not to stumble over His controversial reputation but to believe the miracles as proof that He was from God. If you don't understand what is going on in your life right now, then remember the good things God has done in the past that prove His love and faithfulness. Perhaps this would be a good time to review your own testimonies of God's faithfulness in your life. **With whom can you share a testimony today? Will you allow those testimonies to encourage you today?**

4. **John 10:40-42**—Then Jesus went back across the Jordan to the place where John had been baptizing in the early days. Here he stayed and many people came to him. They said, "Though John never performed a miraculous sign, all that John said about this man was true." And in that place many **believed** in Jesus.

• John baptized in a remote spot. Having been to Israel on nine occasions, I can picture how desolate it truly was. The people had to make a special effort to get to John or Jesus. Sometimes you must work diligently to get to a place of faith as well. God will not always make faith convenient. **Is that true in your life right now? Does it seem like more effort than it should?**

• Notice how logical their faith was; they thought it through and decided to believe. **Where can faith be a logical conclusion for you?** Faith can involve feeling but in most cases, it is a rational conclusion based on the facts. God is faithful, and you choose to believe that and act accordingly.

———◦•◦———

5. **John 11:14-15**—So then he told them plainly, "Lazarus is dead, and for your sake I am glad I was not there, so that you may **believe.** But let us go to him."

• The disciples still needed their faith bolstered. They had seen so much but still needed to see something more. **Are you honest with God about your faith level, or are you faking it, as if God doesn't know the truth?**

• Jesus knew and accepted that the people needed to see more proof of His power. God helps us grow in faith and sets up situations that will cause our faith to increase. He truly is the author and finisher of our faith (see Hebrews 12:1-2).

———◦•◦———

6. **John 11:25-27**—Jesus said to her, "I am the resurrection and the life. He who **believes** in me will live, even though he dies; and whoever lives and **believes** in me will never die. Do you **believe** this?" "Yes, Lord," she told him, "I **believe** that you are the Christ, the Son of God, who was to come into the world."

• We have conquered death through Christ. We will live even if we die! Hallelujah!

• Mary's confession was a powerful one for a Jew to make.

She had faith; therefore, she spoke faith (see 2 Corinthians 4:13-14).

• Jesus got specific with Martha. He asked her point-blank if she believed that He was who He said He was. Jesus may be confronting you too. **Do you believe He is who He said He is? Do you believe that He is the resurrection and the life?**

• Faith is the means to eternal life. I had a seminary professor who defined eternal life as a quality of life so good and pure that nothing could cause it to end. So your faith is the means by which you obtain this quality of life. Think about your faith testimonies. **Aren't they a great way to live? Don't they bring you joy just to think of them? How would you like to live in a constant state of joy?** Then look for ways to use your faith to generate more testimonies!

• Having faith in Jesus means you have faith in all that He teaches as well.

⸻

7. **John 11:40**—Then Jesus said, "Did I not tell you that if you **believed**, you would see the glory of God?"

• If you have faith, you will see God's glory and excellence.

• Glory isn't a radiant light or some supernatural manifestation. It is God's goodness revealed in the midst of the human condition. God's glory in this context was shown as Jesus raised Lazarus from the dead. **Where have you already seen God's glory in your own life or experience? How can you give a testimony to that glory?**

⸻

8. John 11:42-48—"I knew that you always hear me, but I said this for the benefit of the people standing here, that they may **believe** that you sent me." When he had said this, Jesus called in a loud voice, "Lazarus, come out!" The dead man came out, his hands and feet wrapped with strips of linen, and a cloth around his face. Jesus said to them, "Take off the grave clothes and let him go." Therefore many of the Jews who had come to visit Mary, and had seen what Jesus did, put their **faith** in him.

But some of them went to the Pharisees and told them what Jesus had done. Then the chief priests and the Pharisees called a meeting of the Sanhedrin. "What are we accomplishing?" they asked. "Here is this man performing many miraculous signs. If we let him go on like this, everyone will **believe** in him, and then the Romans will come and take away both our place and our nation."

• Lazarus died and was dead for days for the benefit of others, so they could believe. **What has the Lord put you through for the benefit of others? Does God have the right to do that?** Yes, if you have surrendered your life to Him. He can use you as an example for and to others.

• The chief priest felt he had to protect the nation by opposing Jesus. By doing that, he actually confirmed that the Jews would lose their nation, the very thing they wanted to save. Faith is the only way to please God. These leaders did not have faith for Israel. Instead, they saw themselves as Israel's, and in a sense God's, caretakers. Their lack of faith, or should I say faith in their nation, caused them to kill God, the one who had given them the nation in the first place. This sealed Israel's fate.

9. **John 11:43-45**—When he had said this, Jesus called in a loud voice, "Lazarus, come out!" The dead man came out, his hands and feet wrapped with strips of linen, and a cloth around his face. Jesus said to them, "Take off the grave clothes and let him go." Therefore many of the Jews who had come to visit Mary, and had seen what Jesus did, put their **faith in** him.

• Here is an instance of miracle-producing faith. I don't think anyone had faith for Lazarus to come back to life (except Jesus), or even considered it much of a possibility. God went beyond what the people thought was possible. I must never think that my faith controls God or is the only means by which He can act. God is a free agent and can act as He sees fit! Yet my faith seems to provide a platform, a reason even, for Him to do something great.

• Jesus delayed in coming, and that allowed Lazarus to die. **Has something happened to you for which there is no explanation? Could it have easily been prevented had God only acted in a more timely manner? Could it be that God is using you and your situation to increase others' faith as they watch what He does in your life? Are you willing to be an encouragement to others as your own faith is stretched and tested?**

• **For what did the people have faith after Lazarus was raised?** Many had faith that Jesus was the Messiah. That faith evaporated in just a few days, however, when Jesus hung to die on the cross. They could not comprehend how their glorious Messiah, a descendant of David, and one who could raise the dead, could allow such a thing to happen. At one point, their faith was high; a few days later, it was shattered. **Has that ever**

happened to you? What steps can you take to make your faith more consistent?

———————

10. **John 12:10-11**—So the chief priests made plans to kill Lazarus as well, for on account of him many of the Jews were going over to Jesus and putting their **faith** in him.

• Not everyone is happy when you have faith, especially if it challenges another person's own religious system that supposedly has God all figured out.

• These priests were going to undo what God had already done. They were going to kill Lazarus after Jesus had raised him from the dead! There may be some who dedicate themselves to tearing down what your faith has built up. Don't let them discourage you. Keep on trusting!

• These priests were part of a religious-political system; they saw that they were losing their constituency and had to do something to protect their position and interests. They were willing to resort to murder and actually did when they killed Jesus.

• Some people are disturbed when you make a decision to "go over to Jesus" or to "put your faith in Him." **Is anyone angry with you right now because of your faith? Are you willing to endure their anger to trust God?**

———————

12. **John 12:36**—"Put your **trust** in the light while you have it, so that you may become sons of light." When he had finished speaking, Jesus left and hid himself from them.

• Jesus seemed to imply that you become like the focus of your faith. If your faith is in capitalism, you will be a capitalist. If your faith is in Buddha, you will become like the spirit of Buddha. If you put your faith in Jesus, the Light, then you will be a son of the Light. We become like what we trust. So if you lack Christlike character in any area, it may be a deficiency of faith. "I have a bad temper" or "I could never be that holy" are really statements that lack faith. You don't have the faith that God can help you be who He wants you to be. **Does this make sense? In what area of your life is there a lack of faith that is showing up as some character flaw?**

• The people did not believe in Jesus after all He had done for them. Therefore, He withdrew from them. Lack of faith causes God to move on. (**Remember when Jesus left his hometown of Nazareth, unable to perform miracles there due to their unbelief?** See Matthew 13:53-58.)

13. **John 12:37-43**—Even after Jesus had done all these miraculous signs in their presence, they still would not **believe** in him. This was to fulfill the word of Isaiah the prophet: "Lord, who has **believed** our message and to whom has the arm of the Lord been revealed?" For this reason they could not **believe**, because, as Isaiah says elsewhere: "He has blinded their eyes and deadened their hearts, so they can neither see with their eyes, nor understand with their hearts, nor turn—and I would heal them." Isaiah said this because he saw Jesus' glory and spoke about him. Yet at the same time many even among the leaders **believed** in him. But because of the Pharisees they would not confess their **faith** for fear they would be put out of the synagogue; for they loved praise from men more than praise from God.

• *Not* to put your faith in Jesus is *not* to believe in God Himself! **How can someone say, "I believe in God," but reject the One He sent?** That isn't possible. God does not want people who simply believe He exists but those who believe *and* do His will.

• The prophet Isaiah saw Jesus' glory, had faith, and spoke about it—700 years before Jesus was born! **What do you see today? Are you talking about it?** Remember what Paul wrote: "It is written: 'I believed; therefore I have spoken.' With that same spirit of faith we also believe and therefore speak" (2 Corinthians 4:13).

• This is a difficult passage. **How can anyone believe in God if God has blinded their eyes and deadened their hearts?** It seems, however, that their hearts were so set against God that God turned them over to their own hardness! In Exodus, it says that Pharaoh hardened his heart and then God hardened it (see Exodus 7:3, 8:19, and 9:12). **Does this make sense? Would God do something like that?**

• The writer of Hebrews encourages us *not* to harden our hearts. **Why?** Because we can get to the point where God helps the hardening process along! **Have you hardened your heart in any area?** Ask the Lord to show you. Don't stay in your hardness, or you risk God hardening your heart for you (see Hebrews 3:12-13).

⸺⸙⸺

14. **John 12:42-44**—Yet at the same time many even among the leaders **believed** in him. But because of the Pharisees they would not confess their **faith** for fear they would be put out of the synagogue; for they loved

praise from men more than praise from God. Then Jesus cried out, "When a man **believes** in me, he does not **believe** in me only, but in the one who sent me."

• Not all the leaders were against Jesus. Many in their hearts had put their trust in Him. Their faith, however, was incomplete because they did not confess it. Their love for their culture and way of life was greater than their love of God. **Do you love your church more than you love Jesus? What about your denomination or your religious traditions?**

• **Is your church affiliation working for you or against you in your faith walk? If it is against you, what are you prepared to do?** You are here to please God, not your church, its leaders, or your denomination.

• **Faith is not faith unless it is publicly stated—is that a fair statement?** There is something missing when you don't declare what you believe. The Jewish culture did not allow the leaders (or the people) to confess their faith in Jesus because the synagogue had become such an important part of their lives.

• There is praise from God that I don't always wait for, work for, or want. It's not as "public" as praise from other people. **Are you working for the praise that comes from God? How do you know?**

• If God wants you to do something, do it, no matter what people say or how it makes you look in their eyes.

• There are some who insist that there are many ways to God. Jesus said if you don't believe in Him, then you don't believe in God, the one who sent Him. This is a difficult statement for those in our politically correct culture to accept. It can cause you to be silent when you should speak this truth. **Have you been silenced by the tolerant spirit of this age?** It is interesting that our culture is tolerant of everything and everyone, except those who are intolerant!

15. **John 12:46**—"I have come into the world as a light, so that no one who **believes** in me should stay in darkness."

• Guidance should not be a problem for you and me. If we want to do God's will, then He must show us the light and show us what that will is. Jesus lights our way. We cannot be held accountable for what we do not now.

• If you truly want to know God's will, then commit to do it *before* you know what it is; He will then reveal it to you. Abandon your veto power to God's will, and He will show you what it is (see John 7:17). That involves great faith. You trust Him so much that you promise to do anything He asks *before* you know what it is. **Can you say, "Lord, show me Your will. I'll do whatever it is"?**

16. **John 13:19**—"I am telling you now before it happens, so that when it does happen you will **believe** that I am He."

• In a previous passage above, God was working to blind the people to faith. Here He is working to stimulate and encourage the faith of His followers. I don't know about you, but I want God working with and for me, not against me.

• If your heart is set toward faith, God will help you. If it isn't, He can actually provide situations that will discourage your faith from growing. I want to have a heart of faith and allow God to help it grow. There is only one way for faith to grow, and that is to walk through the challenging times that allow God to prove His faithfulness.

• Many times, God opened the eyes of His followers to see what was right there in front of them all along. **What aren't you seeing right now?** Ask God to open your eyes to see what you're not seeing, something that will encourage your faith.

---

17. **John 14:1**—"Do not let your hearts be troubled. **Trust** in God; **trust** also in me."

• **So if my heart is troubled, am I *not* trusting God about some issue? What do you think? Is that true in your life?**

• Jesus sounded as though it was a decision to maintain a troubled heart. If your heart is anxious, you can make a decision to make it un-anxious? Worry and anxiety are decisions. **Do you agree? Are you anxious?** Then you can decide not to be. If you decide not to worry, then you can decide to trust as well.

---

18. **John 14:10-11**—"Don't you **believe** that I am in the Father, and that the Father is in me? The words I say to you are not just my own. Rather, it is the Father, living in me, who is doing his work. **Believe** me when I say that I am in the Father and the Father is in me; or at least **believe** on the evidence of the miracles themselves."

• Jesus was encouraging the disciples to focus their faith on the miracles if they could not understand everything else He was saying at that time. I have mentioned this before, but it bears repeating: it is crucial that you see and remember the miracles and faithfulness of God. Those things will encourage you in the dark, difficult faith times that we all must endure. **What acts of yesterday have you forgotten about that can help your faith today?**

• Stop right now and make a list of the ways God has been good to you. **What has He done for you? What testimonies do you have of times when you had faith and God provided, delivered, saved, or healed?** If you can't hear or understand what He is saying today, then at least hold on to what He has done—"the miracles themselves."

———————

19. **John 14:12-13**—"I tell you the truth, anyone who has **faith** in me will do what I have been doing. He will do even greater things than these, because I am going to the Father. And I will do whatever you ask in my name, so that the Son may bring glory to the Father."

• Jesus had to assure the people that He was telling the truth. Why? What He had to say, which was normal, was abnormal compared to the subnormal spirituality of the day. He went on to say that *anyone* with faith in Him would do greater things than He had done. **Why do I only consider that "something greater" to be raising the dead or some other dramatic miraculous manifestation? Do you share that thinking?**

• Jesus never wrote a book, founded a hospital or school, planted a church, started a business, or adopted a child. All those enterprises are miracles in and of themselves. God helps people to accomplish those actions because they have faith in Him. Those achievements could be the greater works that Jesus referred to in this verse. **Do you agree or disagree with that line of thinking?**

• Some people yearn for the "greater things" and, because they don't see what they think are the greater things, become disillusioned with the Church or God's people. Yet people are doing greater things every day, and their faith is what allows them to do so. **What is blocking your faith from doing greater things than Jesus did?**

• **What greater things can you do for God that doesn't involve raising the dead or feeding the multitudes? What is within your gifting to do for God? Could you build an orphanage? Adopt a child? Take a missions trip?** Once you determine what it is, go and do it in faith.

———

20. **John 14:29**—"I have told you now before it happens, so that when it does happen you will **believe.**"

• God is always speaking and communicating. **Are you listening? What is He saying?** He speaks through His Word, circumstances, people (believers and unbelievers), nature, and with the still, small voice in your heart. If I were with you right now, sitting across from you, I would ask, **"What is God saying to you these days?" What would you answer?**

• **If you had no answer, is it that God isn't speaking or you're not listening? Do you think that your humanity is big enough to stop the God of the universe from communicating**

with you? I doubt it. You can ignore God, but you can't stop Him from speaking!

• God speaks to increase our faith. Remember what Paul wrote in Romans: "Consequently, faith comes from hearing the message, and the message is heard through the word of Christ" (Romans 10:17). God can speak through others or by the still, small voice inside of you. In whatever way He speaks, it is so your faith can grow.

• That is why it's so important to hear His voice in whatever way He may be speaking to you. **Do you keep a journal of what God is saying to you? If not, this would be a good time to start one, don't you think?**

━━━━➤●◄━━━━

21. **John 16:8-9**—"When he comes, he will convict the world of guilt in regard to sin and righteousness and judgment: in regard to sin, because men do not **believe** in me."

• The Holy Spirit has come to convince men and women that they are sinning or "missing the mark" if they do not believe in Jesus. It isn't my job to convince them; it is the Holy Spirit's job. I just bring the words, but God the Spirit has to work in their lives and hearts.

• This means that you don't have to strive to convince people of the truth, although you need to take advantage of every opportunity you have to do so. You never know when the Spirit will use you to convince someone else that Jesus is Lord. **Are you taking advantage of every opportunity you have to present the truth, leaving room for the Holy Spirit to convict** the listeners? How are you presenting the truth—in a judgmental way, or with love, compassion, and faith?

———>●<———

22. **John 16:27**—"No, the Father himself loves you because you have loved me and have **believed** that I came from God."

• **Is this saying that God's love is conditional upon our having faith in Jesus?** I thought God loved everyone.

• **Is loving Jesus and having faith in Jesus connected somehow?** I think it is. As I stated earlier, God isn't interested in those who give intellectual or mental assent to His existence. God loves those who believe in Jesus and choose to obey Him.

———>●<———

23. **John 16:30-31**—"Now we can see that you know all things and that you do not even need to have anyone ask you questions. This makes us **believe** that you came from God." "You **believe** at last!" Jesus answered.

• It was three and a half years, and the disciples finally believed! Hallelujah! I'm no different. It has taken me a lot longer to believe God about some things.

• You and I need to be patient with those who are working out their own faith, whether for salvation, job or relationship changes, or some other aspect of daily life. We need to encourage faith, not demand it. We need to give examples of faith from our own lives and allow the Spirit to teach people the truth. **Are you relying on the Spirit to convict and convince others, or are you trying to be the Holy Spirit to other people?**

• You need to be patient with yourself as your own faith grows. Five years ago, I wanted to start my own business, but I wasn't ready. My faith wasn't sufficient, and I was afraid. Today I'm ready, and it has been wonderful. It took me some time, however, to get there. **What are you nurturing your faith to be able to do eventually?**

———————

24. **John 17:8**—"For I gave them the words you gave me and they accepted them. They knew with certainty that I came from you, and they **believed** that you sent me."

• The disciples believed in Jesus' mission; they had faith that He had come from God. **Do you have faith that what is happening in your life at the moment is from God? If not, where did it come from?** Either God is in control or He isn't.

• If you can accept Jesus' words, you can also reject them. It is a choice, not a feeling. **Have you accepted Jesus' words in every area of your life?**

• Faith is the assurance of things hoped for, so you can believe and know with certainty. You must first believe, however! (See Hebrews 11:1.)

———————

25. **John 17:20-21**—"My prayer is not for them alone. I pray also for those who will **believe** in me through their message, that all of them may be one, Father, just as you are in me and I am in you. May they also be in us so that the world may **believe** that you have sent me."

• Jesus prayed for those who believe to be one with Him and

the Father. What a prayer! **What does it mean?** I'm not sure I know what it means to be one with the Father and Son in the Spirit. It sounds so grand, almost too good to be true.

• That's it—we can be one "in the Spirit!" That's how we can be one—by maintaining the unity of the Spirit! I don't think I ever saw that until I wrote it just now. Thank you, Lord!

• We cannot be one by trying to agree on this issue or that one. Our unity must be a spiritual unity. That is, the Spirit must maintain it. It is as if I have a power cord to my heart and mind, and I must plug that cord not into you, my church, or my doctrine. I must plug that cord into the Spirit, and that source will help me maintain my unity with you because that is where you are "plugged in." **Does that make sense?** This unity is something I cannot achieve without God's help.

• **Are you walking out your unity with your brothers and sisters in Christ? Do you talk well of them? Do you give them the benefit of the doubt when there is an issue on which you may not agree?** Remember what Paul wrote: "Make every effort to keep the unity of the Spirit through the bond of peace" (Ephesians 4:3).

———————

26. **John 19:35**—The man who saw it has given testimony, and his testimony is true. He knows that he tells the truth, and he testifies so that you also may **believe**.

• I should tell truthful testimonies so that others may believe. I have, at times, exaggerated my stories, hoping that people will believe. That isn't necessary. I am making an effort to ensure that the stories and examples I use when I teach are accurate and not embellished. **I want my testimony to be true, don't you?**

• Earlier I asked you to sit down and list your faith stories. **Did you follow through?** If you haven't done that yet, please do so now. John wrote down the testimony of what he saw, and 2,000 years later, it's still helping people to believe. Your testimonies and stories have power. Write them down, publish and broadcast them. I am not equating your testimonies with John's inspired word of God; but they still have power, and God can use them. First, however, you have to do your part. **What are you waiting for?** Start writing!

———

27. John 20:8—Finally the other disciple, who had reached the tomb first, also went inside. He saw and **believed**.

• **Do you believe that God raised Jesus from the dead?** If so, you can believe anything! If you have faith that God raises the dead, you can believe that God heals, provides finances, opens ministry doors, or does any other exceptional feat. Once you accept the resurrection, the hard part of faith is done.

• Churches are filled every Easter Sunday with people who say they believe that a dead man came back to life. **Why can't they believe that God can change their heart or the heart of another person?** After all, that is easier than raising a dead man back to life.

• **What difference does your faith in resurrection life make in your daily walk with the Lord? Shouldn't it make a significant impact on your decisions?** When I lay hands on a sick person, I remember that this sickness, as difficult as it may be from my perspective to heal, is not as challenging as raising a dead person. So if I can have faith for the resurrection, I can have faith for healing—my own or for someone else.

• Having placed your faith in the fact of Jesus' resurrection means that you can have faith for your own resurrection. Hallelujah!

———⟫♦⟪———

28. **John 20:25-31**—So the other disciples told him, "We have seen the Lord!" But he said to them, "Unless I see the nail marks in his hands and put my finger where the nails were, and put my hand into his side, I will not **believe** it." A week later his disciples were in the house again, and Thomas was with them. Though the doors were locked, Jesus came and stood among them and said, "Peace be with you!" Then he said to Thomas, "Put your finger here; see my hands. Reach out your hand and put it into my side. Stop doubting and **believe**." Thomas said to him, "My Lord and my God!" Then Jesus told him, "Because you have seen me, you have **believed**; blessed are those who have not seen and yet have **believed**." Jesus did many other miraculous signs in the presence of his disciples, which are not recorded in this book. But these are written that you may **believe** that Jesus is the Christ, the Son of God, and that by **believing** you may have life in his name.

• John wrote his gospel so that people would believe that Jesus was (and is) the Son of God. It's good to have a purpose for whatever you do. My purpose in writing *The Faith Files* is to increase your faith for daily living.

• Jesus gave Thomas the proof that He needed. If you want to believe, God will give you the proof you need, although not necessarily the proof for which you ask. By that, I mean that He may not give you the "sign" you ask for, but if you're looking, you will know that what you see is an answer to your prayer.

• One day while discouraged over my finances, I asked God for a specific amount of money. Later that day, at a public amusement park with my family, some people I didn't know gave me free tickets and food. I didn't get the money I asked for, but I saw that the Lord was able to provide. He chose to give me those things and not what I asked for as an answer to my prayer. I accepted those things as from Him, not insisting that my prayer be answered in the way I wanted, and I took it as a sign that God was encouraging my faith that day. Later he gave me the full answer to my prayer, but on that day, I received tickets and hot dogs. **Are you looking past today's faith encouragement because it isn't the full answer you are seeking?**

• **What do you need from God so that you may have faith?** Ask Him; go on, ask Him. Stop being proud or foolish. If you need faith help, ask, just as Thomas did. Then believe that He will answer your prayer for help—but not necessarily in a way that you expect. After all, you have to receive God's faith encouragements in faith!

———

CONCLUSION

Congratulations! You have reached the end of *The Faith Files*. **What did you learn from John's gospel about faith? What changes are you going to make as a result of what you learned?** Once you determine your action plan from John's gospel of faith, then you are ready to move on to the final word that finishes up this study but not your faith journey.

FINAL THOUGHTS
ON APPLYING YOUR FAITH

I hope you know a little more about your faith now that you have finished this volume of *The Faith Files*. More importantly, I hope you have decided what to do because you have faith.

In my book, *Life Is a Gold Mine: Can You Dig it?*, I mentioned the possibility of studying what Jesus and Paul had to say about faith. That is where I got the idea for this series of books called *The Faith Files*. Before we finish this volume and I move on to the next, however, I thought I would include some other ideas from *Life Is a Gold Mine,* just in case you still need some additional help in ways to apply your faith to daily life. Here they are:

Is your giving all that it can be? What do you have that you no longer use that you can give away now? What percent or amount of your income would you like to give away in the next 12 months? Can you give some time to volunteer?

Can you believe God for time? If so, what you can you do that you have been putting off because you believed you didn't have time? Now that you believe you do, can you write the book, compose the song, start the business, earn the degree, or make the missions trip?

Review your purpose in light of what you have read. Where are you thinking small about who you are and what you can accomplish?

Identify one hero of faith in the Bible who can stir you to act on your purpose. Study their life with a view to emulating their faith.

One of the recurring themes of this volume is found in 2 Corinthians 4:13: "With that same spirit of faith, we also believe and therefore speak." **Write down negative confessions you make regularly**, things like "I'm no good at that," or "God could never use me to do this," or "I could never afford that." Once you have written them down, go out and burn the list and determine to start adjusting your words to correspond with your faith.

Review your list of goals. You have a list, don't you? If not, perhaps you should start by composing one. Then review the list. Can you accomplish your goals in your own strength? If so, where does faith enter this equation? Perhaps you need to enlarge some of your goals. You don't have to know today how you will accomplish your goals tomorrow.

What are you believing for at the present time that, if God doesn't help you, you will fail or look bad trying? If you don't have such a project or goal, is your faith really being stretched and applied to your daily life?

With whom can you apply what you've learned from *The Faith Files*? Where can you teach some of the things God taught you about faith? Can you start a faith support group that will encourage the members and hold them accountable for faith results?

Who would benefit from a copy of *The Faith Files?* Why not give them a copy today or for the next special occasion in their life?

It has been an honor to share with you these thoughts on faith. Be watching for future editions of *The Faith Files* that will focus on faith studies in the other New Testament books. If I can help you in any way, or if you have an insight or a question to include in future *Faith Files* projects, don't hesitate to contact me at johnstanko@att.net. Until the next volume, I pray that you will bring great pleasure to God's heart as you apply what you have learned about faith in faith.

———————

About the Author

John Stanko is the founder and president of PurposeQuest International, which creates resources and tools to help people around the world clarify their purpose and order their world. He is a sought-after conference speaker and consultant and his website and blog are popular sites where people go to better understand who they are and how they can be more productive. John resides in Pittsburgh, PA and is currently pursuing a Doctor of Ministry degree from Reformed Presbyterian Theological Seminary while he continues to write and compile future volumes of *The Faith Files*.

You can stay in touch with John's world through the following sites:

www.purposequest.com • www.johnstanko.us
www.stankomondaymemo.com • www.faithfiles.net
www.stankobiblestudy.com (where you can subscribe
to receive his weekly Bible studies)
or via email at johnstanko@att.net

PurposeQuest International
PO Box 91099 • Pittsburgh, PA 15221-7099
1.412.646.2780

www.ingramcontent.com/pod-product-compliance
Lightning Source LLC
Chambersburg PA
CBHW070106070426
42448CB00038B/1826